CHARLESTON
F1RSTS

ALSO BY MARK R. JONES
& EAST ATLANTIC PUBLISHING

Doin' the Charleston: Black Roots of American Popular Music
& the Jenkins Orphanage Legacy
(2013)

Kingdom By The Sea: Edgar Allan Poe's Charleston Tales
(2013)

OTHER BOOKS

Palmetto Predators: Monsters Among Us
(2007)

South Carolina Killers: Crimes of Passion
(2007)

Wicked Charleston, Vol. II: Prostitutes, Politics & Prohibition
(2006)

Wicked Charleston: The Dark Side of the Holy City
(2005)

CHARLESTON F1RSTS

Mark R. Jones

EAST ATLANTIC
EAP.
PUBLISHING

First Edition

First Printing 2015

ISBN: 978-0692359525

Cover & book design by Mark R. Jones

Front cover photos: Courtesy Library of Congress

Back cover photos: Courtesy Library of Congress

Printed in the United States of America

TABLE OF CONTENTS

Introduction   9

COLONIAL CHARLESTOWN FIRSTS: 1670-1780
1. English Walled City   11
2. Rice Planted   13
3. Public Library   15
4. Female Artist   17
5. American To Receive A Medical Degree   18
6. Opera Performed   19
7. Theater Built   20
8. Fire Insurance Company   22
9. Scientific Weather Observations   24
10. Female Newspaper Publisher & Editor   26
11. Successful Indigo Crop   28
12. Private Musical Society   31
13. Statue Erected of a Public Figure   34
14. Chamber of Commerce   39
15. Natural History Museum   43
16. Independent Flag to Replace the Union Jack   46
17. South Carolina Revolutionary War Battle   50
18. Plan of Government   52
19. Decisive Victory of the Revolution   54
20. American Imprisoned in the Tower of London   60

ANTEBELLUM CHARLESTON FIRSTS: 1781 – 1865
21. Golf Club In America   65

22. American to Petition for a Copyright 68
23. Public Orphan House 71
24. Scottish Rite Masonic Lodge in the World 83
25. Couple to Honeymoon at Niagara Falls 87
26. Public Fireproof Building 89
27. Reformed Society of Israelites 97
28. Introduction of the Poinsettia 99
29. Regularly Scheduled Passenger Train Service 104
30. Fatality on an American Railroad 108
31. Children's Newspaper Published 109
32. Municipal College 114
33. State To Secede 118
34. Shot of the War Between the States 134
35. Successful Submarine Attack 160
36. Memorial Day Celebration 179

MODERN CHARLESTON FIRSTS: 1866 – 2015

37. Black Associate Justice of a State Supreme Court 185
38. Municipal Historic Zoning Ordinance 190
39. American Folk Opera 195

Bibliography 211
About the Author 216

As always.

for Kari and Rebel

INTRODUCTION

In 2014, for the fourth year in a row, Charleston was named the #1 city in America by *Conde Nast Traveler*. *Travel + Leisure* named Charleston the best city in the United States and Canada for the third consecutive year. Being first is not out of the ordinary for this extraordinary city. Charleston has a long list of revolutionary events and pioneering accomplishments.

When you search the phrase "Charleston Firsts" online, you will discover hundreds of websites that have a list, most of them similar or an exact copy of the previous one, with a lot of cut-and-paste used in their creation. (Hopefully, by the time you purchase it, this book will the #1 item your search reveals.)

Many of the entries in these online lists are cryptic, asserting a "fact" but providing no historical proof. As a Charleston tour guide and historian, I am often exposed to someone - tourist, local or another guide - reciting one of these "firsts." Knowing that Charleston's history is often viewed through sepia-toned glasses, I decided to put some of them to the test, to see how they might stand up to the harsh light of scrutiny.

Using those online compilations, I made a master list of more than sixty "firsts" associated with Charleston. My goal was to discover enough historic material to make a case for each event. Some of these "firsts" were slam-dunks – first state to secede, first shot of the War Between the States. Others proved to be false – the first dry ice was *not* manufactured in Charleston – and one could not be verified - the first rivet-less cargo ship.

Some of these entries are short – less than 1000 words, and a few are much longer. The historic story behind each "first" dictated the length.

Many people know that South Carolina was the first state to secede, but are not aware of the fascinating events leading up to that event. Likewise the stories of the first shot of the War (Between the States) and the first submarine to sink an enemy ship, are long and detailed.

Aimed at the "casual lover" of history - not those interested in reading dry, academic recitation of facts - anyone who reads these stories in order will be able to understand why Charleston is called "America's Most Historic City."

A note: The spelling of the city is used in proper historic context: "Charles Town" before 1719; "Charlestown" from 1720-1783; and "Charleston" after 1783.

Mark R. Jones
April 12, 2015
Charleston, SC

1 1694 FIRST ENGLISH WALLED CITY IN NORTH AMERICA

In 1680 the Carolina capital was officially established on the peninsula between the Ashley and Coopers rivers – the present location of Charleston. The colonists soon began constructing some rudimentary fortifications along the eastern, Cooper River side of town.

In 1686 Jean Boyd created a hand-drawn map of Charles Town, the earliest one known. He depicted two "forts" on the eastern waterfront along Bay Street, connected by a linear entrenchment.

The South Carolina Commons House of Assembly passed an act in 1694 that appropriated money for the construction of a brick wall along the city's eastern edge "to prevent the sea's further encroachment."

Two years later the Assembly appropriated more money for a "wharf wall," or "curtain line upon the Bay." In December it was decided to build a "fortress Battery or fortification … at ye Point of Sand Northward of ye Creek commonly called Collins his creek." This was located north of the eastern end of present-day Water Street and was named Granville Bastion.

In 1703 Gov. Nathaniel Johnson encouraged the Assembly to pass an act for repairing the existing fortifications and building new works to surround the town. This law specified that

> the severall forts, halfe moons, platforms, batterys and flankers, built . . . on the front wall [i.e., East Bay Street], shall have gabions fixed upon them, and shall also be well piled, [for] their preservation against the sea," while the fortifications to be built along modern Water, Meeting, and Cumberland Streets "shall be [made] by

intrenchments, flankers and parapets, sally ports, a gate, drawbridge and blind necessary for the same.

This plan created a ring of fortifications surrounding sixty-two acres of higher ground, which included four corner bastions linked by curtain walls and eight redans. One year later Gov. Johnson reported that the entrenchments were "in great measure perfected."

Cropped section of the 1711 Edward Crisp map of Charles Town, Illustrating the walled fortifications. *Courtesy Library of Congress*

2 1695   FIRST RICE PLANTED IN THE COLONIES

Enterprising Carolina colonists were the first to cultivate rice in America and it began quite by accident. According to tradition, in 1685 a storm-battered ship sailing from Madagascar limped into the Charles Town harbor. To repay the kindness of the colonists for ship repairs, the captain made a gift of a small quantity of "Golden Seed Rice" (named for its color) to the community.

The low-lying marshlands bordered by fresh tidewater rivers along the coast of the Carolinas and Georgia proved ideal for rice cultivation. The soils were rich, reasonably flat and highly fertile. They also were so soft that a man could hardly stand on them. With twice a day tides pushing fresh water onto the flood plains, nothing else could be grown there. By 1700 rice was established as a major colonial crop. That year 300 tons of rice, referred to as "Carolina Gold Rice," were shipped to England.

The labor-intensive requirements of rice cultivation are often credited as the main force behind the creation of the plantation system in the South. With the ox and mule-drawn equipment of the times, rice plantations of few several hundred acres required 100 to 300 laborers to prepare the soil, plant, weed, reap, thresh and winnow their production - all by hand.

By 1726, the Charles Town was exporting about 4,500 tons of "Carolina Gold," which later became the standard of high-quality rice in Europe. According to the Collector of Customs in Charlestown, there was so much rice that "there were not enough ships in the harbor to export it all." When America gained its independence fifty years later, rice became one of the country's major agricultural enterprises.

South Carolina Lowcountry rice fields. *Courtesy Library of Congress*

3 1700   FIRST PUBLIC LIBRARY IN THE COLONIES

A law passed by the South Carolina Commons House of Assembly on November 16, 1700, established a provincial library in Charles Town and provided for its governance. The institution was founded by the Reverend Thomas Bray with the Proprietors and wealthy citizens making contributions to the library. All citizens could borrow books.

The library was located on St. Philip's Street, on a plot of John Coming's original land grant from the Proprietors. It was part of the glebe lands given to the English church by Coming's widow, Affra Halreston.

The library operated out of St. Philip's church parsonage on this site for fourteen years. After the parsonage was relocated, the site was used for various commercial enterprises. In 1858 a girls' school was established on the site, which is currently occupied by Memminger Elementary School.

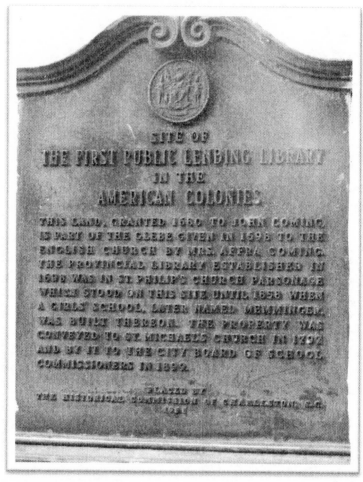

Marker on St. Philip's Street, on the wall near the entrance to the girls' high school – present day Memminger Elementary School. *Photo by author*

4 1707   FIRST FEMALE ARTIST
IN THE COLONIES

Henrietta Johnston was born in France, to Huguenot parents who moved to London in 1687. In 1694 she married Robert Dering and moved to Ireland where she began to draw pastels, depicting a number of important people she was related to by marriage.

In 1704 Robert Dering died, leaving Henrietta with two daughters. One year later she married Anglican minister Gideon Johnston who, in 1707, was appointed as commissary of the Church of England in North Carolina, South Carolina and the Bahamas. Johnston also served as rector at St. Philip's Church in Charles Town.

Johnston's salary payments were often delayed, and in a letter written in 1709, Johnston stated that "were it not for the assistance my wife gives by drawing of Pictures (which can last but a little time in a place so ill peopled) I should not be able to live," indicating that Henrietta had again taken up her drawing to augment the couple's income.

Between the years 1707-1728, Henrietta Johnston painted pastel portraits of such wealthy Charlestonians as Lt. Gov. Thomas Broughton, Sir Nathaniel Johnson, and Col. William Rhett.

According to *American Colonial Portraits* by Richard Saunders and Ellen Miles, Henrietta Johnston was the earliest recorded female artist and first known pastelist working in the English colonies.

5 1734 FIRST NATIVE-BORN AMERICAN TO RECEIVE A MEDICAL DEGREE

William Bull II was born September 10, 1710, at Ashley Hall Plantation, the home of his father. The elder Bull was a large land owner, surveyor and served as acting governor and lieutenant governor of South Carolina for seventeen years.

The younger Bull was educated in England and then at Leiden University in the Dutch Republic (present day Netherlands) where he received his Medical Doctor degree on August 18, 1734. Returning to South Carolina he did not establish a medical practice. Instead, he became a planter and, like his father, served as lieutenant governor (1759-1775) and on five different occasions acting governor. His final term began in March 1773 when Governor Montagu left for England. Bull served as acting governor until June 18, 1775 when Lord William Campbell became South Carolina's last royal governor.

In 1777 Bull refused to take the oath of allegiance to the Revolutionary government and left for England, He returned to Charlestown in February 1781 during the British occupation of the city and served on the Board of Police. When the British troops evacuated Charlestown at the end of the Revolutionary War Bull returned to England where he died in 1791.

6 1735 FIRST OPERA PERFORMED IN THE COLONIES

On February 18, 1735, the ballad opera *Flora, or Hob in the Well* was performed at Shepheard's Tavern in Charlestown. Local musicians provided accompaniment and sang. The play is often mistakenly attributed to Colley Cibber, an English actor, playwright and Poet Laureate. The real truth is rather involved.

The comic character Hob, the farm boy, was first created in 1696 by the Restoration comedian Thomas Doggett for his five-act comedy *The Country Wake*. Hob was reborn in a 1720 condensed adaptation of *The Country Wake*: titled *Hob; or, the Country-wake*. Nine years later John Hippisley reworked the piece as a ballad opera and retitled it after the heroine of the plot: *Flora; an opera, or, Hob in the Well*.

In the spring of 2010, the newly remodeled Dock Street Theater revived the opera as a highlight of Charleston's Spoleto festival, in a production directed and designed by John Pascoe, with a score based on the original tunes by American scholar-composer Neely Bruce.

7 1736   FIRST THEATER BUILT IN THE COLONIES

Sited on the corner of Church and Dock Streets (now known as Queen Street), the Dock Street Theatre was the first building in America constructed specifically to be used for theatrical performances. On February 12, 1736, the Dock Street Theatre opened with a performance of *The Recruiting Officer,* a 1706 comedic play by Irish writer George Farquhar. The second work featured in the theater was the ballad opera, *Flora, of Hob in the Well* after its successful premiere the year before at Shepheard's Tavern.

The original Dock Street was destroyed by a fire in 1796, and in 1809 the Planter's Hotel was constructed on the same site. In 1835 the wrought iron balcony and sandstone columns of the Church Street facade were added. The Planter's became one of the finest hotels in the South. Most histories of Charleston claim that the famous drink, Planter's Punch, was first served here, but that is not true. The recipe originated in Jamaica and was most likely brought to Charleston from the Caribbean.

After the War Between the States, the Planter's Hotel fell into disrepair and was slated for demolition. But in 1935, the original building became a Depression Era Works Progress Administration project. The hotel's grand foyer became the one for the new theatre and the hotel dining room now serves as the box office lobby.

On March 18, 2010, the Dock Street Theatre reopened after a three year, $19 million dollar renovation by the City of Charleston which included state-of-the-art lighting and sound, modern heating and air conditioning.

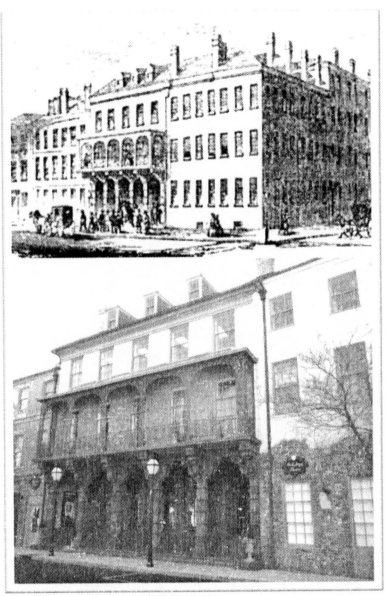

Top: Planter's Hotel, newspaper advertisement, circa 1830s. *Author's collection.*
Bottom: Dock Street Theater, 2014. *Photo by author.*

8 1736 FIRST FIRE INSURANCE COMPANY ESTABLISHED IN THE COLONIES

In 1736 the "Friendly Society for the Mutual Insuring of Houses Against Fire at Charles Town" was organized but proved to be short-lived. Four years later, the devastating Great Fire of 1740 destroyed over 300 buildings and bankrupted the company.

In 1752 Benjamin Franklin brought together a group of Philadelphians to create The Philadelphia Contributionship for the Insurance of Houses from Loss by Fire. Franklin's business was more successful, and is often cited as the first fire insurance company, although established sixteen years after Charlestown's ill-fated Friendly Society.

At one point Charlestown had more than a dozen fire insurance companies that issued metal fire markers to policyholders which signified their property was insured against fire damage. For owners the markers served as proof of insurance. For insurance companies, it served as a form of advertising, and alerted volunteer firefighters that the property was insured.

According to local legend, a fire company would not extinguish the flames in a building without a marker since they would not be paid. This is false. Charlestown ordinances required all fire companies to respond to all conflagrations. There was, however, a reward system for the first company on the scene, paid for by the city.

Today you will see "fire mark plaques" on buildings throughout the city. Most of them are reproductions.

Fire markers on various Charleston buildings. *Photos by author.*

9 1738 FIRST SCIENTIFIC WEATHER OBSERVATIONS IN THE COLONIES

Twenty-two-year old Dr. John Lining arrived in Charlestown from Lanarkshire, Scotland in 1730. He quickly became concerned with the epidemics that plagued the area. Lining claimed they "came regularly at their stated seasons like a good Clock." Charlestown was only two years removed from a major yellow fever epidemic.

In January 1738, Dr. Lining began to study weather conditions to determine if and how they effected human health. From his home, he began the first weather observations made with scientific instruments and systematically reported, on the American continent. He recorded temperature, rainfall, atmospheric pressure, humidity, wind direction and speed in an attempt to establish a connection between weather and disease. During that year two more plagues swept across the lowcountry, yellow fever and small pox killed more than 10 per cent of the population.

In 1742 Lining mentioned his scientific observations in a letter to his friend Charles Pinckney then living in London. Pinckney forwarded those letters to the Secretary of the Royal Society and were published in the *Philosophical Transactions of the Royal Society,* which raised Dr. Lining's standing among scientists around the world.

Dr. Lining also conducted experiments to

> discover the Influence of our different Seasons upon the Human Body ... [to] arrive at some more certain knowledge of the cause of our Epidemic Diseases.

Lining corresponded with Benjamin Franklin on the subject of electricity and carried out his famous kite and key experiment during a local thunderstorm. Lining also made studies of yellow fever and wrote one of the first published scientific accounts of that disease in North America - *A Description of the American Yellow fever, Which Prevailed at Charlestown, in South Carolina, in the Year 1748.*

The results of Dr. Lining's experiments were published in the *Transactions of the Royal Society of London* and in *Gentleman's Magazine.*

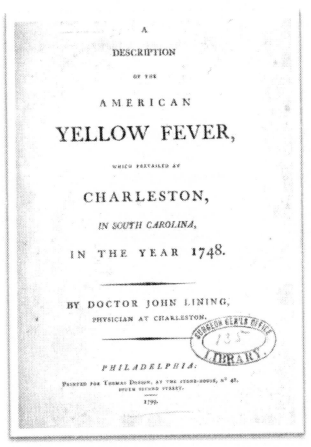

Cover of Dr. Lining's yellow fever paper, reprinted in 1799. *Author's collection.*

10 1738 FIRST FEMALE NEWSPAPER PUBLISHER & EDITOR IN THE COLONIES

Following the death of her husband Lewis, Elizabeth Timothy continued to fulfill the partnership agreement Lewis had signed with Benjamin Franklin to purchase the *South Carolina Gazette*, making her the first female newspaper publisher and editor in America.

On January 4, 1738, in her initial edition, Timothy appealed to her readers:

> Whereas the late Printer of this Gazette hath been deprived of his life, by an unhappy accident, I take this Opportunity of informing the Publick that I shall continue the said Paper as usual; and hope, by the Alliance of my Friends, to make it as entertaining and correct as may be reasonably expected. Wherefore I flatter myself, that all of Persons, who by Subscription or otherwise, assisted my late Husband, on the Prosecution of the said Undertaking, will be kindly pleased to continue their Favors and good Offices to his poor afflicted Widow and six small children and another hourly expected.

Elizabeth operated the *Gazette* under the name of her 13-year-old son, Peter. As the official printer for the province, the Timothys printed acts and other proceedings for the Assembly, as well as books, pamphlets and tracts.

When Peter Timothy reached the age of 21, his mother relinquished control to him. Before and during the American Revolution Peter used the paper to promote the Patriot cause. In August 1780 he was arrested by the British and exiled to St. Augustine, Florida.

Years later, in his famous autobiography, Benjamin Franklin praised Elizabeth's business acumen, writing that she

> operated the Printing House with Reguarity and Exactitude ... and manag'd the Business with such Success that she not only brought up reputably a Family of Children, but at the Expiration of her Term was able to Purchase of me the Printing House and establish her Son in it.

In 1973 Elizabeth Timothy was inducted into the South Carolina Press Association Hall of Fame.

Historic marker on the corner of East Bay and Vendue Range, Charleston.
Photo by author.

11 1741 FIRST INDIGO CROP HARVESTED IN AMERICAN COLONIES

Elizabeth (Eliza) Lucas was born in Antigua, West Indies in 1722, the oldest of four children. She was provided a formal education at a finishing school in England. Her father, George Lucas, moved the family to the South Carolina colony in 1738, hoping the climate would be more suited to the health needs of his ailing wife. George inherited several plantations near Charlestown, one of 600 acres near Wappoo Creek and the other a 1,500-acre parcel at Garden Hill.

An intelligent young woman with an insatiable curiosity, Eliza mastered the writings of Milton, Virgil and Locke, spoke fluent French and played the flute. She also studied botany and became interested in plants that were compatible with the Carolina lowcountry climate. When recalled to his post in Antigua, Lucas left his plantations in the capable hands of his 17-year old daughter, Eliza.

Eliza was determined to grow an indigo crop on her Wappoo Plantation. The indigo plant was used to create a natural blue dye, rare at that time, and highly prized in the developing textile industry in England. Because of the difficulty in its production, the English were grudgingly forced to buy it from France. Since small quantities of indigo was grown in parts of the British West Indies Eliza was convinced it could become profitable in South Carolina.

Her father sent indigo seeds to Eliza, and aided by their slaves, many of whom may have had experience with the plant in the Caribbean, she began to cultivate indigo. Over several seasons, she developed a new strain compatible to the Carolina climate.

To help produce the dye into cake forms George Lucas hired Patrick Cromwell, a professional dye maker from the British island of Montserrat. He helped Eliza produce six pounds of dye stuff, which was shipped to England. The Carolina dye was found to be superior to the French-made indigo and Eliza began to share her seeds and techniques with planters throughout the Lowcountry. Within three years more than 100,000 pounds of indigo were shipped to England, making it second only to rice as the colony's most important crop and accounted for more than one-third of all South Carolina exports.

Historian Edward McCrady described Eliza's importance to the Carolina economy in an exuberant and exaggerated manner:

> Indigo proved more really beneficial to Carolina than the mines of Mexico or Peru were to Spain ... The source of this great wealth ... was a result of an experiment by a mere girl.

By the age of twenty-one this "mere girl," was successful, independent and became the target of dozens of would-be suitors. She ultimately fell in love with and married Charles Pinckney, twenty years her senior, a successful lawyer and former Speaker of the Common House of Assembly. On their plantation Eliza experimented with hemp and flax. She also raised silkworms and briefly revived silk production in South Carolina. Eliza and Charles had three children who survived into adulthood including two sons who became national figures:

- ✝ CHARLES COTESWORTH, served as a Revolutionary War officer, signed the U.S. Constitution, ran as Federalist vice-presidential candidate in 1800 and the party's Presidential candidate in 1804 & 1808.
- ✝ THOMAS, served as a Revolutionary War officer, and was elected South Carolina governor in 1787. In 1792 he was appointed Minister to Great Britain by George Washington and in 1795 served as Envoy Extraordinary to Spain where he negotiated the Treaty of San Lorenzo, also known as Pinckney's Treaty. He was also the Federalist vice-presidential candidate in 1796.

Eliza Lucas Pinckney died of cancer on May 26, 1793 in Philadelphia and was buried there at St. Peter's Church. Her legacy of determination and innovation earned her such renown that President George Washington asked to serve as one of her pallbearers.

She was inducted in the South Carolina Business Hall of Fame in 1989, the first woman to be so honored.

12 1766   FIRST PRIVATE MUSICAL SOCIETY IN THE COLONIES

Charles Fraser, Charleston lawyer and painter, wrote in 1854:

> The love of music was an early characteristic of the people of Charleston, and very generally cultivated by them as an accomplishment. Out of this grew the St. Cecelia Society, originally an association of gentleman amateurs, who met together to indulge a common taste and to pass an agreeable hour. It afterward increased in numbers and resources.

The tradition of private concert patronage was part of the cultural heritage brought from Europe. With its mixture of English, French, Scottish, Irish and German immigrants, a rich legacy of music was obviously part of Charleston's cultural life. Since much of that culture was a reflection of English and Scottish folkways, the establishment of a "private subscription music society" was a logical step.

The loss of the early records of the St. Cecilia Society due to the Great Fire of 1861, have thwarted detailed research about the Society's history. However, it is known that on St. Cecilia's Day, November 22, 1737, a concert of vocal and instrumental music, organized by Charles Theodore Pachelbel, was performed in Charlestown.

There are several sources that claim 1762 as the founding year of the Society, although the first newspaper notices about its activities appear in 1766. The *South Carolina and Georgia Almanack* for 1793 also includes a listing which states unequivocally that the St. Cecilia Society was "formed in 1766."

St. Cecilia was the patroness of musicians. *Author's collection.*

Furthermore, on November 22, 1866, the first meeting of the Society after the Civil War was announced as "The Centennial Anniversary Meeting of This Society." The 1762 date seems to come from an error from Robert Mills' *Statistics of South Carolina* published in 1826.

Four of the founding members - Benjamin Yarnold, Thomas Pike, Peter Valton and Anthony L'Abbe - were professional musicians who all performed concerts at the City Theater on Queen Street. They also performed benefit concerts to raise money for a new organ at St. Michael's Church.

Sometime in April 1766, these musicians, with other notable gentlemen, most of whom were amateur musicians, formed the Society at the corner of Broad and Church streets in Robert Dillon's Tavern (later called the City Tavern).

The Society was incorporated in 1784 and in 1819 the board of managers reported that they:

> had found it impracticable to procure an orchestra for the Society, and therefore ordered a ball to be given. After that, one more effort was made to obtain

performers, when the committee reported to the Society
that they could only procure a quinette.

Over the span of fifty-four years (1766–1820), the Society
presented forty-three seasons of regular concerts. The eleven years
of inactivity were mainly the result of the American Revolution,
the War of 1812 and financial downturns.

In 1822 the concerts were discontinued and the Society
substituted dancing assemblies, which have continued into the 21st
century.

From the beginning, the Society concerts were open only to
members and their guests, and that tradition continues to this day.
It has never been a public institution. For the past century, the
Society has also limited its membership to the male descendants of
earlier members, which has closed the organization to anyone
without deep roots in Charleston.

FOUNDING MEMBERS OF THE
ST. CECILIA SOCIETY OF CHARLESTON
NOVEMBER 22, 1766

Thomas Bee	John Gordon	Henry Peronneau
Donald Bruce	George Abbott Hall	Thomas Pike
James Carson	Benjamin Huger	William Pillans
William Carson	Issac Huger	Charles Cotesworth Pinckney
William Crabb	Anthony L'Abbe	Owen Roberts
James Crallan	Edward Lightwood, Jr.	Alexander Rose
William Ward Crosthwaite	Lachlan McIntosh	George Roupell
John Deas	Arthur Middleton	Thomas Shirley
William Henry Drayton	John Moultrie	Roger Smith
Barnard Elliott	Thomas Moultrie	Thomas Loughton Smith
Alexander Fraser	David Oliphant	Peter Valton
Alexander Garden		

13 1770 FIRST STATUE ERECTED OF A PUBLIC FIGURE IN THE COLONIES

William Pitt, former British secretary of state and a leader in the House of Commons, gave a speech in Parliament on January 14, 1766, in support of the American colonies' opposition to the Stamp Act.

> Gentlemen, Sir,
> I have been charged with giving birth to sedition in America. They have spoken their sentiments with freedom against this unhappy act, and *that* freedom has become their crime. America is almost in open rebellion.
> I rejoice that America has resisted.

Pitt proposed that the Act be repealed and several weeks later, when his speech became news in America, he was cheered as a hero.

Although in ill health, a few months later Pitt was asked by the king to form a government. He appointed Charles Townshend as Chancellor of the Exchequer, in charge of collecting and managing taxes and other revenues. Due to his infirmities, Pitt struggled to maintain support in the Commons and was negligent in his management of the government.

Charles Townsend took advantage of Pitt's weakness and pushed the so-called Townsend Revenue Act through Parliament, which imposed duties on glass, lead, paints, paper and tea imported into the colonies. Townshend hoped the act would defray expenses in the colonies, but many Americans viewed the taxation as an abuse of power, which resulted in organizing the colonies for a common goal – a boycotts on British imports.

In May 1766 the news reached Charlestown that Parliament had repealed the Stamp Act and the city celebrated by ringing church bells and burning bonfires. The Assembly voted £1000 sterling to commission a marble statue of William Pitt in "gratitude of his exertions for the repeal of the Stamp Act."

Four years later, on May 31, 1770, the statue of William Pitt arrived in Charlestown at Charles Elliott's Wharf aboard the *Carolina Packet* from London. Its arrival created great public excitement. Cannons were fired to attract attention, and crowds gathered to cheer as it was unloaded. Citizens "of the highest rank" carried it by hand "to the Arsenal near the place where it is intended to be erected." The Arsenal was located on the southwest corner of Broad and Meeting streets, present day location of the U.S. Post Office.

The bells of St. Michaels were supposed to be rung "but were stopped out of regard to Issac Mazyck, a very worthy member of the community, who was extremely ill near the church."

On July 5, 1770 the statue of William Pitt - the first to commemorate a public figure in America - was dedicated in the intersection of Meeting and Broad Streets. It was placed upon a pedestal designed by John and Peter Horlbeck. Peter Manigault publicly read the inscription:

> In grateful memory of his services to his country in general and to America in particular, the Commons House of Assembly of South Carolina unanimously voted this statue of the Hon. William Pitt, Esq. who gloriously exerted himself by defending the freedom of Americans, the true sons of England, by promoting a repeal of the Stamp Act in the year 1766. Time will sooner destroy this mark of their esteem than erase from their minds their just sense of his patriotic virtue.

A flag that read "Pitt and Liberty" was raised and members of the Club Forty-five led the crowd in three "hurrahs!" That evening Club Forty-five hosted a party at Mr. Dillon's Tavern where forty-five toasts were drunk.

Club Forty-five was organized a few months earilier at Dillon's tavern in support of John Wilkes, publisher of *The North Briton*. Wilkes had published an article (in edition # 45) critical of

King George III's close friend, Prime Minister John Stuart. Wilkes considered Stuart an incompetent idiot and said so in *North Briton #45*. When the King decided to prosecute Wilkes for seditious libel, his cause became a rallying cry for freedom throughout the colonies.

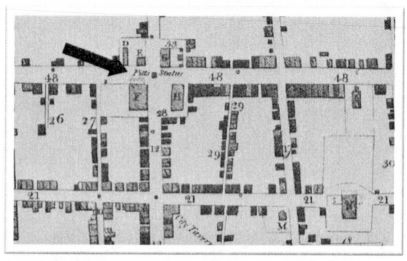

Iconography of Charleston, 1788 for the Phoenix Fire Insurance Company, with the arrow indicating the location of the William Pitt in the intersection of Broad and Meeting Streets. *Courtesy Library of Congress.*

Through the years the Pitt statue has endured an interesting, and often inglorious, history.

On April 17, 1780, a British cannonball, fired from a James Island battery, shot off the extended left arm of the statue. After the war the statue was considered a nuisance and impediment of traffic in one of the city's busiest intersections and City Council had it moved in 1794. As it was being removed from its pedestal the statue's head broke off. Judge John Grimké purchased the marble pedestal and placed the inscription slab in his garden at 321 East Bay Street. The rest of the statue's pieces were "stowed away in some of the public buildings."

By 1808 the statue was erected on the grounds of the Charleston Orphan House, facing Calhoun Street. Judge Grimké returned the original inscription and it was erected with the statue. In 1881 the

South Carolina Historical Society requested that the statue be moved to the newly redesigned Washington Park, behind City Hall.

In 1985 the statue was placed in the lobby of the Charleston Museum as a conservation effort. Finally, in 2002, the William Pitt statue was moved to the lobby of the Charleston County Judicial Center, about 1000 feet from its original location at Meeting and Broad streets.

Current location of the Pitt statue, entrance of the Charleston County Judicial Center at 100 Broad Street. *Photo by author.*

14 1773 FIRST CHAMBER OF COMMERCE ESTABLISHED IN THE COLONIES

On December 9, 1773, the Charlestown Chamber of Commerce was organized at Mrs. Swallows' Tavern on Broad Street.

The formation of the Chamber can be traced back to the economic stress the British Empire suffered after the Seven Years' War (the French and Indian War). The victory over the French had come at a high cost, so Parliament passed the 1764 Sugar Acts and the 1765 Stamp Act in an attempt to pay the debt run up during the war. The Stamp Act required that most printed materials in the colonies be produced on "stamped paper" – an embossed revenue mark. Those included newspapers, legal documents, playing cards and magazines.

There was quick and passionate opposition in Boston, New York, Philadelphia and Charlestown. Leaders throughout the colonies argued that only their representative assemblies could levy taxes against the citizens – no taxation without representation. Violence against British stamp commissioners took place in most of the major towns in America. Charlestown was no exception.

In October 1765 the *Planter's Adventure* arrived in Charlestown, carrying the hated British stamps, in preparation of the Act taking effect in November. Lt. Gov. Bull first placed the stamped paper aboard the warship *Speedwell,* but feared it might be attacked while docked. He secretly transferred the stamps to Ft. Johnson for safekeeping.

Meanwhile in town, a forty-foot-high gallows was erected by outraged locals at Broad and Church streets, in front of Dillon's Tavern. The gallows included three effigies: that of a stamp distributor hung between a Devil on one side and a boot on the other.

On the front of the gallows was a sign: "LIBERTY and no STAMP ACT." On the back of the gallows was a second sign, which read:

> Whoever shall dare attempt to pull down these effigies had better been born with a mill stone about his neck, and cast into the sea.

Unsure of the stamps' location, two thousand people paraded in the streets. The home of the stamp officer, George Saxby, was searched and ransacked. The mob then marched to the "New Barracks" (present-day location of the College of Charleston), burned an effigy of Saxby and buried a coffin labeled ÁMERICAN LIBERTY."

An armed mob of "about 60 to 80" marched on Henry Laurens' house at midnight, suspecting he held the stamps. Lauren's coolness toward the Patriot cause at this time made him subject to suspicion in the eyes of the public. He later wrote that the mob held "a brace of cutlasses across my breast" and for the next hour his house was searched. Laurens was amazed by the lack of damage to his house:

> Is it not amazing that such a number of Men many of them heated with Liquor & all armed with Cutlasses & Clubbs did not do one penny damage to my Garden not even to walk over a Bed & not damage to my Fence, gate or House?

For the next week a mob marched the streets daily, threatening to kill the two stamp agents George Saxby and Caleb Lloyd unless they resigned. The two besieged agents, in fear for their lives, publicly promised not to perform their assigned duties.

Parliament repealed the Stamp Act at the urging of William Pitt in the spring of 1766 but then passed the Declaratory Act, which stated that Parliament's authority was the same in America as Britain and asserted its authority to pass laws that were binding on the thirteen colonies. Then on June 29, 1767 Parliament passed the Townshend Revenue Acts, placing new duties on paper, paint, lead, glass, and tea that were imported into the colonies. The tax had far-reaching effect on the economy Great Britain and the colonies.

Three years later, after more unrest among the colonists, the Townsend Acts were repealed by Parliament. But in an effort to avoid the appearance of weakness in the face of intense colonial protest, the tea tax was left in place. This allowed the East India Company to export tea tax-free to the American colonies.

On January 17, 1774, Charlestown received word of the Boston Tea Party, and that Boston merchants were calling for all colonies to cut off all trade with Britain in order to force a repeal of the Tea Act. Most Charleston merchants and political leaders supported the boycott.

"A View of Charles-Town, the Capital of South Carolina" by Thomas Leitch, 1774.
Cropped to illustrate the Exchange Building on East Bay Street.
Courtesy Library of Congress.

On the first day of December 257 chests of tea arrived in Charlestown on the ship *London* igniting a crisis. Handbills were passed out, calling for a mass meeting of all South Carolinians in the great hall of the newly constructed Exchange Building.

Two days later, December 3, the meeting demanded that the tea be sent back to England and resolved to boycott the businesses of anyone who refused to sign its boycott petition. The meeting also resolved not to purchase any tea being taxed to raise revenue in America. The petition stated:

> We the underwritten, do hereby agree not to import, either directly or indirectly, any teas that will pay the present duty, laid by an act of the British Parliament for the purpose of raising a revenue in America.

Anonymous letters were sent to the London captain and the wharf owner threatening to burn both the ship and its mooring site.

It was within this volatile atmosphere of political upheaval and business uncertainty on December 9, that a group of Charleston men, most likely many of the same ones who had attended the meeting at the Exchange, met at Mrs. Swallows Tavern and organized the Chamber of Commerce. Today it is called the Charleston Metro Chamber of Commerce and is the longest continually operating business membership association in the United States.

15 1773 FIRST NATURAL HISTORY MUSEUM IN THE COLONIES

Inspired by the British Museum, the Charleston Museum was established on January 12, making it the first in America.

The Charlestown Library Society provided the core collection of natural history artifacts for founding the Museum. Residents were encouraged to donate objects for the new institution on Chalmers Street. Some of initial acquisitions included "a drawing of the head of a bird, an Indian hatchet, a Hawaiian woven helmet, and a Cassava basket from Surinam."

The museum also acquired "a Rittenhouse orrery, a Manigault telescope, a Camera obscura, a hydrostatic balance, and a pair of elegant globes."

The museum ran the following ad:

THE MUSEUM OF SOUTH CAROLINA
IN CHALMERS' STREET (near the City Square)

Consisting of an extensive collection of Beasts, Birds, Reptiles, Fishes, Warlike Arms, Dresses and other CURIOSITIES – among which are:

The Head of a New Zealand Chief
An Egyptian Mummy (a child)
The Great White Bear of Greenland
The South American Lion
The Duck Bill'd Platypus from new Holland
The Bones of an Ostrich as large as those of a Horse
The Boa Constrictor or Anaconda Snake, 25 feet long
The Grampus Whale, 20 feet long

800 Birds, 70 Beasts, 200 Fishes
Shoes of the Chinese Ladies, 4 inches long
The Saw Fish, saw 4 ½ feet in length
A large collection of views of the Public buildings, etc.
in Europe
A Fine Electrical Machine

The whole elegantly arranged in glass cases, open every day from 9 o'clock, and brilliantly illuminated every evening with occasionally a Band of Music.

The museum was also home to the only known fossil of the extinct *Pelagornis sandersi,* which is the largest flying bird ever discovered.

The Museum operated as part of the private Library Society until 1824 when it opened to the public. In 1852 Harvard scientist Louis Aggasiz declared the museum collection to be "among the finest in America."

During the Civil War, its operation was suspended but in 1907, the collection moved to the Thompson Auditorium at 121 Rutledge Avenue. The 8,000 seat auditorium had been hastily built in 1899 for the United Confederate Veterans reunion and served as the Museum's home until 1980 when the move to the current Meeting Street location was completed.

Several weeks after the move, the Thompson Auditorium burned to the ground, leaving only the four Corinthian columns, now landmarks at Cannon Park.

TOP: Thompson Auditorium when it housed the Charleston Museum. *Courtesy Library of Congress.* BOTTOM: Columns of the auditorium in Cannon Park on Rutledge Avenue, Charleston. *Photo by author.*

16 1775 FIRST INDEPENDENT FLAG TO REPLACE THE UNION JACK

On September 15, 1775, the first American flag to replace the Union Jack in the American colonies was raised over Fort Johnson in Charlestown.

The dramatic events that led to the flag-raising started on January 11 when South Carolina's First Provincial Congress convened at the Old Exchange. The South Carolina delegates to the First Continental Congress had returned with recommendations to better coordinate the American response to the Coercive Acts - the Stamp Act and Tea Act. The Provincial Congress approved a series of resolutions to bring stability to South Carolina. They resolved:

> That it be recommended by this Congress, to all inhabitants of this colony, that they be diligently attentive in learning the use of arms; and that their officers be requested to train and exercise them at least once a fortnight.

The Council of Safety was created and vested with command of the army, the power to contract debts, to stamp and issue money, and to sign all commissions for the army. By the spring every parish and district in South Carolina had assembled militia companies and several regiments.

The Provincial Congress appointed the "Secret Committee of Five," headed by William Henry Drayton and Arthur Middleton. Immediately, the Committee seized the mail that had arrived from England on the *Swallow*. The official British dispatches made it clear that British authorities would not hesitate to use force to keep or restore order in the colonies.

Contrary to modern reinterpretations, the description of the original
flag, designed by William Moultrie, did not mention the word "Liberty."
Author's Collection

Three months later, April 19, during the Battles of Lexington and Concord in Boston, the British suffered seventy-three killed and 174 wounded and the Patriot "Minutemen" lost 125 men. Ralph Waldo Emerson described it as "the shot heard 'round the world."

On April 26, the "Secret Committee of Five," seized the public gun powder at several magazines, including Hobcaw on the Charleston Neck and the arms in the State House at the corner of Broad and Meeting Streets. In all Carolina patriots stole 800 muskets, 200 cutlasses and 1600 pounds of powder.

On June 17 Lord William Campbell, the new Royal Governor, arrived in Charlestown. Campbell was married to Sarah Izard, from one of South Carolina's most powerful families. He expected his arrival to be greeted with typical fanfare – booming cannons and cheering crowds. However, arriving two weeks after the news of the bloodshed in Boston, with the rising revolutionary passions, he greeted with "sullen silence."

Campbell quickly learned that he was little more than a figurehead due to the power wielded by the Provincial Congress. Campbell was aware of the political rift between the rebel-minded low-country and the backwoods Loyalists in South Carolina. He flooded the backcountry with pamphlets claiming that the Provincial Congress could not be trusted and had taken power illegally.

On September 15 Lord Campbell learned that the Patriot leaders had discovered his machinations. Fearing attack from Revolutionaries in Charlestown, Campbell fled his house on Meeting Street in the early morning hours and boarded the HMS *Tamar*. This effectively ended British rule in South Carolina.

Almost immediately Colonel William Moultrie and Captain Francis Marion led a local militia unit and seized Fort Johnson and its twenty-one guns, with no resistance from the British. Lord Campbell, on board the *Tamar*, watched this action and considered it an overt act of war. The fact that it was done in plain view of two British warships make it particularly galling.

Moultrie was then directed by the Council of Safety to devise a flag. He chose the blue of the 1st and 2nd Regiments' uniforms and the silver crescent which adorned their hats. This flag was raised over Fort Johnson, representing South Carolina's overt defiance of British authority.

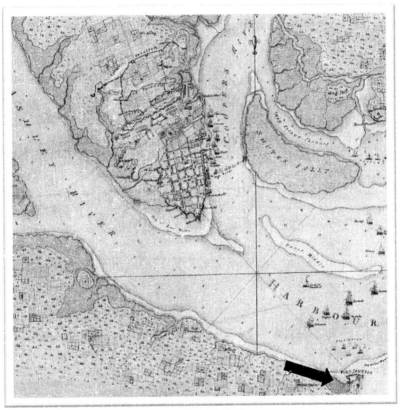

Detail of a map showing Charlestown harbor fortifications, with
Fort Johnson in the lower right hand corner. *Courtesy Library of Congress*

17 1775 FIRST SOUTH CAROLINA MAJOR REVOLUTIONARY NAVAL BATTLE

On November 1 the Second Provincial Congress was hastily called into session to deal with the threat of two British war ships in Charlestown harbor. William Henry Drayton was elected President. In anticipation of Lord William Campbell possibly sailing up the Cooper River to meet with Loyalists living in the back country, Drayton ordered the blocking of Hog Island Channel by the sinking of four hulks.

Ten days later on November 11, South Carolina's first Revolutionary War naval battle took place. Drayton was on board the newly commissioned South Carolina schooner *Defence*, supervising the scuttling of four hulks in the channel, while two British ships, H.M.S. *Tamar* and H.M.S. *Cherokee*, took positions to block the *Defence's* movements. Captain Edward Thornbrough, urged on by Lord Campbell aboard the *Cherokee*, ordered six shots fired. Drayton replied with his nine-pounders.

Over the next several hours the British fired 130 ineffective shots, which rallied support to the revolutionary side. By nightfall the Carolina Patriots were able to sink three of the hulks, effectively blocking the channel.

William Henry Drayton. *Courtesy Library of Congress*

18 1776 FIRST PLAN OF GOVERNMENT IN THE COLONIES

In early February the South Carolina delegation returned from the Second Continental Congress. Delegate John Rutledge warned that a British attack in the South was probable. Fellow delegate, Christopher Gadsden, presented a copy of Thomas Paine's *Common Sense*, which helped inflame local political sensibilities. He also displayed his "Don't Tread on Me" flag to the Provincial Congress. As recorded in the South Carolina congressional journals, the proclamation read:

> Col. Gadsden presented to the Congress an elegant standard, such as is to be used by the commander in chief of the American Navy; being a yellow field, with a lively representation of a rattlesnake in the middle in the attitude of going to strike and these words underneath, "Don't tread on me."

On March 26, four months before the Declaration of Independence was approved, South Carolina adopted a state constitution, drafted by the Provincial Congress. Although two other colonies had written temporary constitutions, South Carolina was the first to establish a complete plan of government.

John Rutledge was elected as the state's president, Henry Laurens as vice-president and William Henry Drayton as its Chief Justice. The 1776 Constitution was considered a temporary measure until "an accommodation of the unhappy differences between Great Britain and America can be obtained." It gave the president "absolute veto power" over the acts of the legislature.

For the second time in its history, South Carolina had made a change in its government. In 1719 the colony had overthrown the English Lords Proprietors in a "Bloodless Revolution" and now replaced British rule with a local government.

The Gadsden Flag, designed by Christopher Gadsden. *Courtesy Library of Congress*

19 1776 FIRST DECISIVE VICTORY OF THE AMERICAN REVOLUTION

Constructed of palmetto logs and sand, Fort Sullivan was strategically sited at the southern end of Sullivan's Island. On June 28, 1776, despite being outmanned and outgunned, South Carolina militiamen commanded by Col. William Moultrie prevented a British fleet from entering the harbor and held off enemy troops attempting to invade from Long Island (present day Isle of Palms). Ft. Sullivan, a small fort of palmetto logs and sand, located on Sullivan's Island, withstood the fire from the British fleet.

In the spring John Rutledge, president of South Carolina, signed an act that prescribed the death penalty and confiscation of property for anyone aiding the British. Rutledge also appointed 46-year-old Col. William Moultrie to prepare the city's military defense.

Moultrie supervised the building of a "large fort" on Sullivan's Island, the key defensive location that geographically shielded the harbor. Large vessels sailing into the harbor had to cross the Charlestown Bar, a series of submerged sand banks lying about eight miles southeast of the city. A half-dozen channels penetrated the bar, but only the southern pair could be navigated by deep-draft ships. A broad anchorage called Five Fathom Hole lay between the bar and Morris Island. Just a thousand yards north of that shoal stood the newly constructed Fort Sullivan.

During the next several weeks, work gangs cut thousands of spongy palmetto logs throughout the Lowcountry and rafted them across the harbor to Sullivan's Island. The fort's design was described as "an immense pen 500-feet long and 16-feet wide, filled with sand to stop the shot." The workers constructed gun platforms out of two-inch planks and spiked them together.

Fort Sullivan was intended to make an invasion as costly as possible, or, to prevent an invader from landing at all. Since such a fixed defensive position could not reasonably be expected to annihilate the enemy, the fort would have to be backed up by inland troops and a well-armed city.

Fort Sullivan. Engrav'd by Wm. Faden, August 10, 1776. *Courtesy Library of Congress*

Former Royal Governor, Lord William Campbell, had been urging the British to mount a major expedition against South Carolina to crush the rebellion in the South. On June 1 the British fleet, commanded by Peter Parker appeared and "displayed about fifty sail before the town, on the outside of the bar."

Col. Moultrie described their effect on Charlestonians:

> The sight of these vessels alarmed us very much, all was hurry and confusion, the president with his council busy in sending expresses to every part of the country, to hasten down the militia; men running about the town looking for horses, carriages and boats to send their families into the country; and as they were going out through the town gates to go into the country, they met the militia from the country marching into town...

Within a week most of the British ships had crossed the bar and were anchored in Five Fathom Hole. General Sir Henry Clinton delivered a proclamation to the Patriots:

> to entreat and exhort them, as they tender their own happiness and that of their posterity, to return to their duty to our common sovereign.

South Carolina President John Rutledge rejected this plea.

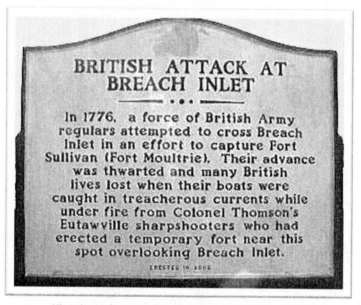

BRITISH ATTACK AT BREACH INLET

In 1776, a force of British Army regulars attempted to cross Breach Inlet in an effort to capture Fort Sullivan (Fort Moultrie). Their advance was thwarted and many British lives lost when their boats were caught in treacherous currents while under fire from Colonel Thomson's Eutawville sharpshooters who had erected a temporary fort near this spot overlooking Breach Inlet.

Historic marker on Sullivan's Island. *Photo by author.*

Upon learning of the presence of Ft. Sullivan, and the fact that the back (land) side of the fort was not completed, Gen. Clinton landed 500 soldiers on Long Island (present-day Isle of Palms) just north of Sullivan's Island. Over the following days, Clinton increased his force on Long Island to almost 3000. His plan was to cross the Breach, an inlet between Long Island and Sullivan's and attack the fort from its unfinished rear while Parker's ships assaulted it from the sea.

Clinton sent a brigade under Maj. Gen. Charles Cornwallis to pitch camp within sight of the Breach. Cornwallis reported that the depth of the Breach at low tide, initially estimated to be only half-a-yard, was in reality seven feet. Col. Moultrie had already stationed an advance guard of 400 men on the other side of the Breach to defend against the crossing, effectively stranding Cornwallis's force.

At 10 A.M. on June 28, nine British warships commanded by Sir Peter Parker attacked Ft. Sullivan. Gen. Moultrie described the situation as "one continual blaze and roar, with clouds of smoke curling over...for hours together."

Outnumbered, with vastly inferior armaments, the South Carolina troops kept the British warships from entering the harbor. At the same time, the 400 men managed to hold the Breach, thwarting British efforts to cross and land troops on Sullivan's Island.

View of Charles Town from on board the *Bristol*. Five Fathom Hole the day after the attack upon Fort Sullivan by the Commodore & his squadron, which action continued 9 hours & 40 minutes. Engrav'd by Wm. Faden, August 10, 1776.
Courtesy Library of Congress.

In the midst of the battle, a British projectile broke the fort's flagstaff. Sgt. William Jasper "leapt over the ramparts" and, shouted, "Don't let us fight without a color!" Jasper, in the words of Captain Horry:

> deliberately walked the whole length of the fort, until he came to the colors on the extremity of the left, when he cut off the same from the mast, and called to me for a sponge staff, and with a thick cord tied on the colors and stuck the staff on the rampart in the sand. The sergeant

fortunately received no hurt, though exposed for a considerable time, to the enemy's fire.

Sgt. Jasper raises the flag over Ft. Sullivan. *Author's collection.*

As American shot bombarded the British men-of-war, one round landed on the *Bristol's* quarterdeck and rendered Sir Peter Parker's "Britches...quite torn off, his backside laid bare, his thigh and knee wounded." The *Acteon* was grounded and severely damaged. By 9 P.M. Parker withdrew and the reports came in:

- † British: 78 dead, 152 wounded. Lord William Campbell was wounded during the battle.
- † American: 12 dead, 25 wounded.

Early the next morning the British set the grounded *Actaeon* afire and abandoned it. The Americans sailed out to the burning ship, boarded it and fired several of its guns at the departing *Bristol*.

The South Carolina soldiers searched Sullivan's Island and "gathered up more shot, from 24-pounders down to the smallest size, than they had fired." The British shot had destroyed almost all of the island's huts and trees, but Ft. Sullivan itself stood almost undamaged. Parker and Clinton evacuated the area in late July and immediately began to blame each other for their defeat.

President Rutledge visited Ft. Sullivan after the battle to congratulate the garrison and give the men a hogshead of rum. For his heroic actions, Rutledge presented his sword to Sergeant Jasper and Col. Moultrie was promoted to general, and Rutledge announced that Ft. Sullivan was to be renamed Fort Moultrie.

It was important to get news of the victory to the Continental Congress as quickly as possible. Normal dispatches often took two or three weeks to reach Philadelphia. Seventeen-year old Daniel Latham, "a very athletic young man," who was a distiller at 1 Hasell Street, set out early in the morning on horseback toward Philadelphia, spreading the good news along the route north. Within a week he arrived in Philadelphia and announced the news of the Sullivan's Island victory to members of the Continental Congress.

It is difficult to over-emphasize the importance of the event. It was so improbable. Fledgling American armed forces had triumphed against one of the worlds' greatest military powers.

In Charleston today, June 28 is celebrated as Carolina Day.

20 1780 FIRST AMERICAN IMPRISONED IN THE TOWER OF LONDON

Henry Laurens was a successful Charleston merchant and planter who amassed one the great fortunes in America. As a partner in the largest slave-trading house in North America, Austin and Laurens, he oversaw the sale of more than 8,000 enslaved Africans during the 1750s. In 1776 he served as Vice-president of South Carolina (see #18) and in 1777 became a member of the Continental Congress. When John Hancock retired on November 1, 1777 due to ill health, Laurens was elected President of Congress and served until December 9, 1778.

After his term as President, Laurens was appointed Minister to the Dutch Republic by the Continental Congress. With his extensive international business contacts, Congress was confident he would be able to procure a loan to help finance the American war effort. In late 1779 he sailed to Holland.

However, during his voyage the British frigate *Vestal* intercepted his ship, the *Mercury*, off the banks of Newfoundland. Laurens tossed his dispatches overboard, but they were retrieved by the British, who discovered the draft of a possible U.S.-Dutch treaty. This prompted Britain to declare war on the Dutch Republic and charge Laurens with treason. He was transported England for trial.

On October 6, 1780 Henry Laurens was confined to the Tower of London for "suspicion of high treason." His imprisonment was vehemently protested by American diplomats to no avail.

During his imprisonment in a Yeoman Warders' house, Laurens's health deteriorated. He was charged rent and board for his rooms and only allowed visitors in the presence of Tower officials.

Henry Laurens. *Courtesy Library of Congress*

Henry Laurens spent the summer of 1781 in the Tower reading Gibbons's *Decline and Fall of the Roman Empire*. He also wrote several letters that drew parallels between Rome and Great Britain and included first-hand accounts of British troops' horrendous conduct in America. These letters were circulated widely in Great Britain and became a source of public embarrassment for Parliament and the King.

On October 9, Henry Laurens's tower guard, Mr. Futerell, presented him with a bill for £97 for his service for one year. Having depleted his funds, Laurens wrote:

> Tis enough to provoke me to change my lodging ... If I were possessed of as many guineas as would fill this room, I would not pay the warders, whom I never employed, and whose attendance I shall be glad to dispense with. Attempts, sir, to tax men without their

consent, have involved this kingdom in a bloody seven years' war. I thought she had long since promised to abandon the project.

On October 19, 1781, Gen. Cornwallis surrendered his British forces at Yorktown, Virginia to Gen. George Washington. This gave American officials some leverage in their attempts to negotiate Laurens's release offering to free Cornwallis from his parole if the Charleston merchant was freed.

Tower of London. *Photo by author.*

Although Laurens was a fellow South Carolinian, and friend, Edward Rutledge argued forcefully against Cornwallis's release. Most South Carolina patriots blamed Cornwallis for the wholesale murder and plundering across the state. Rutledge wrote that Cornwallis should be "held a Prisoner for Life … because he was a Monster and an Enemy to Humanity."

Henry Laurens wrote a bitter note on December 1, which was smuggled from the Tower and sent to Congress:

Almost fifteen months I have been closely confined and inhumanely treated. The treaty for exchange is abortive. There has been languor, and there is neglect somewhere. If I merit your attention, you will not longer delay speedy and efficacious means for my deliverance.

On December 31, Laurens was released, in exchange for Lord Cornwallis and the payment of £12,000 bail bond. He wrote:

On the 31st of December, being, as I had long been, in an extreme ill state of health, unable to rise from my bed, I was carried out of the Tower to the presence of the Lord Chief Justice of England, and admitted to bail "to appear at the court of king's bench on the first day of Easter term, and not to depart thence without leave of the court.

Laurens immediately sent for his daughters, who had been living in France during the War, to join him in London. In an attempt to recover his health, for several weeks he took the waters in Bath. He later helped the American delegation (John Adams, Benjamin Franklin and John Jay) negotiate the Treat of Paris which ended armed hostilities between Great Britain and America.

In a letter to his wife, Abagail, John Adams stated:

I have the Satisfaction to inform you that the definitive Treaties were all Signed yesterday, and the Preliminaries with Holland were Signed the day before. Dr. Franklin has fallen down again with the Gout and Gravel ... Mr. Laurens, has a Brother declining, so that he will go to the south of France, untill he knows his Brother's Fate.

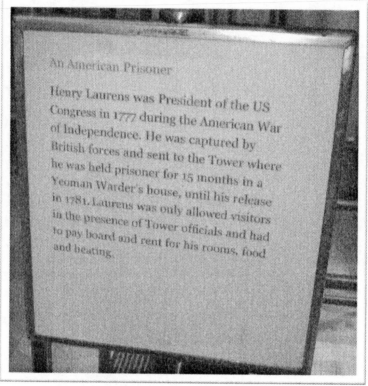

Henry Laurens marker in the Tower. *Photo by author.*

21 1788   FIRST GOLF CLUB IN AMERICA

In 1743 David Deas received the first documented shipment of golf equipment to arrive in the American colonies - 432 balls and 96 clubs sent from the Scottish port Leith to Charlestown. The sheer number is intriguing. During this time, in Europe, most golfers only carried five to eight clubs with them, so this would have been enough to outfit more than a dozen local players, which would lead to the logical assumption the equipment was for more than just Deas's use. That would support the theory that there was already some sort of organized golfing culture in the lowcountry.

Fifteen years later, in 1759, Charleston merchant Andrew Johnston returned from a trip to Scotland with golfing equipment in order to play on his planation. When he died five years later the inventory of his estate listed "twelve goof [golf] sticks and balls."

On May 28, 1788, an advertisement in the Charleston *City Gazette* requested that members of the South Carolina Golf Club meet on "Harleston's Green, this day, the 28th." After which they adjourned to "Williams' Coffee House." Later that year, *The Southern States Emphemris: The North and South Carolina and Georgia Almanac* announced the formation of the South Carolina Golf Club.

Harleston Green was a parcel of undeveloped pastureland on the Charleston peninsula, between Calhoun and Beaufain Streets, stretching from Rutledge Ave to the Ashley River. The Green was often used by locals as a public "pleasure ground" (park).

In 1795 a newspaper notice announced that "The anniversary of the GOLF CLUB will be held on Saturday next at the Club house on Harleston's Green." The last known announcement of a meeting of the South Carolina Golf Club appeared on October 19, 1799.

Some historians suggest that early golf games were played without a set number of holes, no greens and no designated teeing areas. The players dug crude holes in the ground and, since they were unmarked, "finders" (in Charleston they were usually slaves) were sent to stand next to the hole, mark its location and alert others of an approaching shot by hollering "Be forewarned!" After completion of a hole, the player would "tee off at a distance of two club-lengths away from that hole."

The equipment used by these early golfers was rudimentary, to say the least. Wooden clubs were handmade, some crude, others more refined with many looking like modern day hockey sticks. The golf balls of the 1700s were a round piece of cowhide stuffed with goose feathers. Called a "Feathery" they were manufactured while the leather and feathers were wet. As the leather shrunk during the drying process, the feathers created a hard, compact ball. The Feathery was often painted and sold for as much as 5 shillings – the equivalent of twenty dollars in modern currency. At most a Feathery might have lasted two rounds of golf before having to be replaced.

Part of Harleston Green's membership fee requirement was used to "maintain the Green," now called "greens fees."

Ichnography of Charleston, South-Carolina: at the request of Adam Tunno, Esq., for the use of the Phoenix Fire-Company of London, taken from actual survey, 2d August 1788 / by Edmund Petrie. "Harleston Green" highlight added by the author. *Courtesy Library of Congress*

22 1789   FIRST AMERICAN TO PETITION FOR A COPYRIGHT

In January 1774, Dr. David Ramsay arrived in Charlestown from Philadelphia. He was an Irish immigrant, graduate of the College of New Jersey (Princeton), who earned a medical degree from the College of Philadelphia. Within six months Ramsay had established a successful medical practice in Charleston. He was the first physician in town not to have received his medical training in Europe.

Ramsay used two quick avenues for gaining acceptance into Charlestown society: the College of New Jersey and the Congregational Church. Two local friends were former College of New Jersey classmates, Richard Hutson and William Tennant III, minister of the Independent Church. Hutson sponsored Ramsay's membership in the Library Society, which introduced the doctor to some of South Carolina's most prominent men: Gabriel Manigault, Miles Brewton, Christopher Gadsden and Henry Laurens.

During the Revolution Ramsay became an ardent Patriot. On July 4, 1779, he gave a public address in which he stated "our present form of government is everyway preferable to the royal one we have lately renounced."

On May 12, 1780, Charlestown surrendered to the British after a forty-two day siege. Three months later, Ramsay and thirty-three men were arrested and charged with encouraging residents to resist British authority. The prisoners were dragged from their beds and detained in the Exchange Building. Many of them, including Ramsay, were exiled to St. Augustine for several months before they were finally paroled in July 1781.

Dr. David Ramsay. *Courtesy Library of Congress*

After the war Ramsay purchased a home at 92 Broad Street for £3500 and began to research and write his *History of the Revolution in South Carolina,* published on December 7, 1785. Issac Collins of Trenton, New Jersey produced 3200 copies of the book. In order to maximize profits, Ramsay paid for the printing himself. Four years later, he published the *History of the American Revolution.*

On April 4, 1789, Ramsay filed a petition with the House of Representatives, asking Congress to pass a law to grant him the exclusive right of "vending and disposing" of his books within the United States. A Congressional committee approved his petition on April 20, 1789 – making Ramsay the first citizen granted a copyright.

Ramsay's petition to Congress. *Courtesy National Archives.*

23 1790   FIRST AMERICAN PUBLIC ORPHAN HOUSE

When the city of Charleston was incorporated in 1783, the Act of the Legislature also charged the city with the

> care of providing for the poor and educating and maintaining the poor orphan children. And those of poor and disabled parents who are unable to support them.

This shifted the responsibility for these children from the traditional support by the Anglican (English) churches to the city itself.

On October 28, 1790, a Board of Commissioners met to establish rules for the operation of an Orphan House. The original nine commissioners were:

- ✝ John Mitchell
- ✝ John Robertson
- ✝ Richard Cole
- ✝ Thomas Corbett
- ✝ Charles Lining
- ✝ William Marshall
- ✝ Thomas Jones
- ✝ Samuel Beckman
- ✝ Arnoldus Vanderhorst (Indendent/Mayor) of Charleston

The Board was concerned about the expense of providing for the poor children and investigated ways in which to curtail costs. They followed the example of Bethesda Home for Boys in Savannah, a private orphan house established by evangelist George Whitefield in 1740. Consolidating the care of poor children into one facility would mitigate expenses. Older children could be bound out as apprentices with the expense of their care provided by their master. Girls were trained for domestic service, and boys for trade skills such as blacksmithing, carpentry, saddle-making, and printing.

Until a facility could be constructed, the Board's most immediate task was to establish a location to house the children, who at this time, were scattered in various homes across the city. Mrs. Elizabeth Pinckney offered a building on Market Street for children too young to be bound out. However, the location of the building in the unsavory waterfront district, limited its appeal to the Board, and it was looked upon as only a temporary solution. Until the construction of a permanent building in 1794, the Orphan House operated out of several buildings.

Philip Besselleu was hired as a teacher. The goal was to teach basic skills (reading, writing and numbers) to all children. Boys over eight who showed academic skill lived with Mr. Besselleu and were given more strenuous instruction. Sarah Bricken, "a woman of good capacity and character" was hired as the first matron, who was to instruct the girls in sewing and cooking skills. Mr. Vanderhorst provided two slaves (1 male and 1 female) to work in the kitchen. They were to provide the children a decent breakfast (hominy and molasses or mush and butter) and other meals (beef or pork with rice or bread.)

The Board met every Thursday and established a 160-year tradition of a "Commissioner of the Week," rotated among the different members. The Weekly Commissioner was charged with visiting the Orphan House, seeing each child, receiving applications, conducting the Sunday Morning service and reporting his findings to the Board.

On Saturday, May 7, 1791 President George Washington visited the Market Street orphan building, at which there were 107 boys and girls. The President commented that he was impressed with the management of the house.

In 1791, the commissioners estimated the cost for the new building would be £2200. They organized several fund-raising ventures to pay for a new building and operating costs. Local clergy were invited to preach "charity sermons at their respective churches" after which a collection would be taken for the Orphan House. A total of £632 was raised in this manner. By September 1793, total donations from churches, fraternal societies and other groups had reached over £1800.

Thomas Bennett, a local merchant-builder-architect, was given the commission to construct the new Charleston Orphan House on a site at the corner of Calhoun and St. Philip Streets. The four story brick House was the largest structure in the city. It consisted of a center building, 40 by 40 feet, plus two wings 65 by 30 feet each with a cupola on the roof. Boys were to be housed in the East Wing and girls in the West. With only one major renovation, the Orphan House served its purpose for the next 150 years.

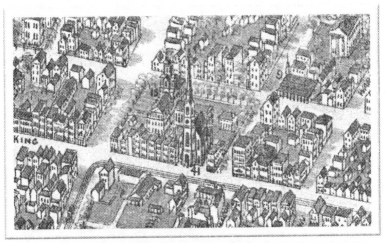

Detail from C. Drie's *Birdseye View of the City of Charleston, South Carolina, 1872.* The Orphan House (15) faces Calhoun Street. St. Matthews Lutheran Church (41) faces King Street. Behind St. Matthews, the small building on the right facing Vanderhorst Street is the Orphan House Chapel.
Library of Congress Geography and Map Division.

On October 18, 1794, the Orphan House opened to 115 children. The opening crowd was so large that it would not fit inside the main building of the Orphan House. The ceremony was conducted twice, once inside the building and a second time on the street for the overflow crowd. Thirteen hundred dollars was raised during the ceremonies. An eight-foot high wall was built around the House's grounds shortly after, financed by a lottery.

Charleston Orphan House, postcard. *Author's collection.*

The first steward (resident manager) was John Wedderspoon. There were four nurses employed: a Mrs. McConnell, Elizabeth Griffiths, Ann McDowell and Mary Brooks. Most of the rest of the work force consisted of slaves. By the early 1800s the House owned ten slaves and nine more had been donated by benefactors.

The Commissioners also created a Board of Lady Visitors to oversee the Matron and nurses. The "Lady Visitors" were required to be "respectable females" – mostly the wives or female relatives of the Commissioners.

In 1802 a chapel, designed and built by local gentleman architect, Gabriel Manigault, was constructed on the grounds behind the House. Local protestant ministers took turns conducting services every Sunday afternoon. Reverend Richard Furman, of Charleston's First Baptist Church, preached the sermon on the opening day, September 19.

Orphan House Chapel on Vanderhorst Street. Orphan House cupola is visible in the background. *Library of Congress.*

During the 1817 fiscal year, the city spent ten per cent of its budget on the Orphan House, about $20,000. It was also supported by private funds and charities, which donated money and food. The Charleston Theater performed an annual benefit performance for the House. Mr. Frederick Kohne, a successful merchant left a bequest of $60,000 and two houses, including a mansion at 91 East Bay Street. Charleston City Council established an endowment for the Orphan House and the Trustees of the Orphan House Funds to manage the endowment. By 1855 the endowment held $64,460, yielding a 7 per cent return.

In 1808 the Orphan House was given a most unusual gift – the statue of William Pitt (see #13), where it remained on the grounds until 1881.

The most commonly cited reason for admission to the Orphan House was poverty. Many of the children were "half orphans," with a single parent who lacked the financial means to rear and support them. The situation of Mrs. Ann Duncan was typical. In her application Mrs. Duncan wrote:

> My husband died on the 18th October 1817 & from his long infirmity expended all his funds & has left me with two children without anything to support us. Necessity compels me to request that you will assist me by taking under your care my daughter Catherine. She is 11 years old.

Over half the children in the House were bound over by their mothers, 11 per cent by their fathers, and about 30 per cent were bound by public officials, such as wardens of the Poor House.

The daily routine for the children was regimented. Boys spent six hours in school, six days a week, 51 weeks of the year. They also spent two and a half hours in private study, one hour and five minutes in washing and dressing and fifty minutes in devotions. The girls were taught writing and arithmetic three hours a day, and then spent three hours and fifty minutes daily in the sewing room and dealing with "household duties."

In 1854, twenty-three year old Miss Agnes K. Irving became Principal of the school. She was trained in the Lancasterian system of education, named after its creator, Joseph Lancaster, which stressed older children teaching the younger. Although the Lancasterian system never became popular in America, it was used at the Orphan House until the 1920s.

Conditions in the House were basic and often lacking. The boys slept on the floor in "two leaky bedrooms ... with only two windows" and the girls shared four bedrooms that were "drenched with water when it rained." Sick children were found to "lie scattered throughout the House in the apartment in which they are taken sick." Since there was little money for candles or lamps, after sunset the Orphan House was cloaked in darkness.

In 1853, a major renovation of the Orphan House was approved. There was pressure on the Commissioners to accept more children so the Orphan House was expanded to allow twice the capacity. Local architects Jones and Lee designed plans for the expansion.

During the Civil War, the Orphan House was visited by Gen. P.G.T. Beauregard who discussed with the Commissioners the possibility that the children may need to be evacuated from the city. At the onset of the Federal bombardment of Charleston in August 1863, the Commissioners realized that removing the children from the city was imperative. A Mr. Legare owned a former ladies seminary one hundred miles north in the town of Orangeburg, South Carolina and offered it for $19,000. George A. Trenholm, a Commissioner and one of the wealthiest men in the South, purchased the building for the Orphan House and the children were moved. When Sherman's troops marched through Orangeburg in early 1865, they spared the seminary building, but sacked the rest of the town. The orphans returned to Charleston at the end of the War.

One of the most distinguished alumni of the Orphan House was Christopher Gustavus Memminger. Admitted at age four as a full orphan he was quickly observed to be "a great native genius, particularly in mathematics."

In October 1813 the nine-year old Memminger was given the honor of addressing the crowd at the celebration of the Orphan House's anniversary ceremony. Thomas Bennett, Jr., son of the Orphan House designer and builder, was impressed with the young lad and informally adopted Memminger and brought him to live in his home in an atmosphere of refinement.

At age twelve, Bennett sponsored Memminger at South Carolina College (the forerunner of the University of South Carolina). Although he was the youngest student at the College, Memminger was singled out for academic excellence. After graduation he returned to Charleston and joined the law office of Joseph Bennett, his benefactor's brother.

Memminger served on the Board of Commissoners at the Orphan House most of his life. He was later elected to the state legislature and as chairman on the Committee of Education, he reformed South Carolina's public school system. For most of his life, he was a passionate proponent of public education. He also served as chairman of the Committee of Finance.

After South Carolina's secession from the Union in 1860, Memminger was appointed head of a committee to compose *The Declaration of the Immediate Causes Which Induce and Justify the Secession of South Carolina from the Federal Union* to explain its reasons for seceding. The declaration stated the primary reasoning behind secession was the "increasing hostility on the part of the non-slaveholding States to the Institution of Slavery."

At the beginning of the war President Jefferson Davis appointed Memminger secretary of the Confederate Treasury, one of the most thankless tasks of the new government. Since the Northern blockade prevented the exportation of cotton, the South's principal economic resource, Memminger developed Treasury policies that proved ineffective against the problems of the Southern states during a four-year war. The Southern economy collapsed and, realizing his job was hopeless, Memminger resigned from office in June 1864.

Christopher Gustavus Memminger. *National Archives*

Memminger took refuge in Flat Rock, N.C., where his summer home had become a wartime haven for friends and relatives. In 1867 he was fully pardoned by President Andrew Johnson, and all of his privileges of citizenship were restored. He returned to Charleston and served in the South Carolina legislature where he endeavored to recover the lost credit of the state and resumed work to improve the South Carolina public school system for whites and blacks.

In 1945 Memminger's Flat Rock home was purchased by Carl Sandburg where the famous poet lived and worked until he died twenty-two years later. In 1969 the home became a National Historic Landmark.

After the War, the Board of Commissioners included some of the prominent men in Charleston, including two wealthy blockade runners, George A. Trenholm and George W. Williams, who became known as the House's "guardian angel." Other members included Christopher Memminger, William C. Bee, Henry A. DeSaussure, Dr. James Moultrie and Dr. Benjamin Huger.

Their service was needed; the years after the War and Reconstruction were some of the most difficult in the Home's history. Charleston was thrown into an economic malaise. Hundreds of children were served, with a peak enrollment of 334 immediately after the War. In 1870, the children were honored by a visit by General Robert E. Lee, who spent a few days in Charleston. The 1886 earthquake damaged the House to the point where the children were forced to live in tents on the grounds for a period while repairs were underway.

Also during this time, an urgent situation developed among a significant portion of the orphaned children in Charleston. Despite its nine decade history of care for white children, it had done little for the African children. Of course, before Emancipation, African children were considered property and most whites completely ignored the suffering of the blacks living under their own roofs. After the War however, hundreds of abandoned black children were living on the streets of Charleston.

Sarah Grimké, who left Charleston as a young woman and became a famous abolitionist in the 1830s, pointed out the double standard among the Charleston white elites. Grimké, who was hated throughout the South as a "traitor" praised the city for providing charity to the white poor, but criticized that they were blind to the fact their wealth and charity was only possible due to a culture based on oppressed slave labor.

The city's first black orphanage was organized in 1891, the Orphan Aid Society, by a black Baptist minister, Rev. Daniel Jenkins. The Jenkins Orphanage, as it came to be known, was never financially supported by the city the way the Orphan House was. (Read the author's 2013 book *Doin' the Charleston: Black Roots of American Popular Music & the Jenkins Orphanage Legacy*.)

By the turn of 20th century, the practice of "binding out" children declined across America during this time and the school expanded their curriculum by adding algebra, typewriting and bookkeeping. The House also boasted one of the best libraries in South Carolina, with more than 5600 books and 1000 pamphlets.

Charleston Orphan House before its demolition in 1953. *Library of Congress*

In 1904 the House received a financial windfall when Andrew Buist Murray, an alumnus, donated $100,000 in honor of his father-in-law, W. Jefferson Bennett. In 1909 President William Howard Taft visited the House and addressed the children, urging them to become productive citizens.

By the 1920s the Home had an endowment of $600,000, the interest of which supplied 40 per cent of its annual budget, the rest being paid by the city and the Duke Endowment. During the 1930s structural repairs to the Home were provided by the Works Progress Administration, including a new roof, a new heating system, and painting the entire structure.

In the years after World War II the Board appointed a Committee to study the mission of the House in the post-War era. They also encouraged a study of the Home by the Child Welfare League of America. The most important recommendation of the Committee and League was the relocation of the Orphan House outside the city for economic reasons.

In 1951 the Commissioners of the Orphan House purchased thirty-seven acres in North Charleston, known as Oak Grove

Plantation, to relocate the children to a more home-like setting. On August 29, 1951 seventy-three children left the Orphan House for the last time and moved to Oak Grove.

The Orphan House building on Calhoun Street was sold to Sears Roebuck and Company for $350,000. Against the protests of the Society for the Preservation of Old Dwellings, the Orphan House and Chapel were demolished in 1953 and replaced by a Sears store.

For the next twenty-seven years, the Charleston Orphan House operated as an agency of the City of Charleston. In 1978 it became an independent non-profit organization known as Carolina Youth Development Center (CYDC), and continues to serve children through nine residential and outreach programs, continuing a 200 year legacy of care.

24 1801 FIRST SCOTTISH RITE MASONIC LODGE IN THE WORLD

On May 31, 1801, the first Supreme Council of the Thirty-third Degree, the Mother Council of the World, was organized in Charleston, with the motto "Ordo ab Chao" (Order from Chaos). Although it is the "Mother Council" for Scottish Rite, it was not the first Masonic activity in the city.

The first Masonic Lodge in Charles Town was established on October 28, 1736. The *South Carolina Gazette* announced:

> Last night a Lodge of the Ancient and Honorable Society of Free and Accepted Masons, was held, for the first time, at Mr. Charles Shepheard's, in Broad Street, when John Hammerton, Esq., Secretary and Receiver General for this Province, was unanimously chosen Master, who was pleased to appoint Mr. Thomas Denne, Senior Warden, Mr. Tho. Harbin, Junior Warden, and Mr. James Gordon, Secretary.

By 1765 there were four active lodges in Charlestown, under the jurisdiction of the Provincial Grand Lodge, and through it, the Grand Lodge of England. They were Solomon's Lodge, Union Lodge, Master's Lodge and Marine Lodge.

The Scottish Rite is one of the two branches of Freemasonry in which a Master Mason may proceed to after he has completed the three degrees of Blue Lodge Masonry – the other branch being the York Rite, which includes the Royal Arch and Knights Templar. The Scottish Rite includes degrees from four to thirty-two.

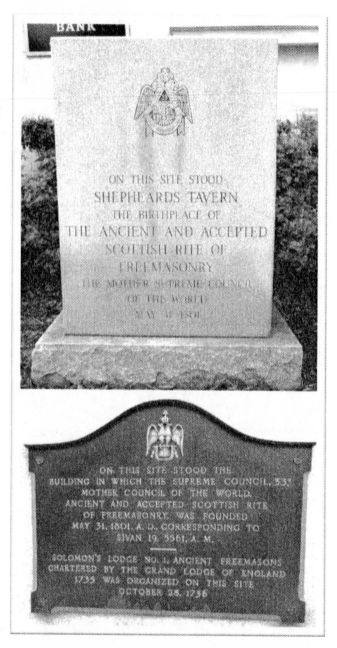

Masonic Markers at Broad and Church Streets, Charleston – the former site of Charles Shepheard's Tavern. *Photos by author.*

The word "Scottish" has led many to believe the Rite originated in Scotland, which is not true. During the mid-1600s many Scots fled to France during the English Civil Wars. The Scots in France who practiced their Masonic interests were referred as "Ecossais," which translates to "Scottish Master."

In 1732 the first "Ecossais" or Scottish Lodge was established in Bordeaux, which included Scottish and English members. In 1763, a Masonic patent was given to Stephen Morin to carry its advanced degrees to America. Morin established his degrees in Jamaica.

In 1801, the Supreme Council was established in Charleston to unify competing groups of "Ecossais." Their membership consisted of eleven Grand Inspectors General:

- John Mitchell
- Frederick Dalcho
- Abraham Alexander
- Emanuel De La Motta
- Thomas Bartholomew Bowen
- Israel De Lieben
- Isaac Auld
- Le Comte Alexandre Francois
- Auguste de Grasse
- Jean Baptiste Marie Delahogue
- Moses Clava Levy
- James Moultrie

The Supreme Council announced control of high-degree Masonry in America by introducing a new system that incorporated all twenty-five of the Order of the Royal Secret, and added eight more, including that of thirty-third degree - Sovereign Grand Inspector General.

It was a diverse group, with only Auld and Moultrie being native-born South Carolinians. Four of the founders were Jews, five were Protestants and two were Catholics. In 1859, under the leadership of Grand Commander Albert Pike, the Supreme Council expanded its membership to the mystical number of thirty-three members.

Pike wrote the *Morals and Dogma of the Ancient and Accepted Scottish Rite of Freemasonry*, a collection of thirty-two essays which provide a philosophical rationale for the degrees of the Ancient and Accepted Scottish Rite. The essays provided a backdrop for each degree with lessons in comparative religion, history and philosophy. His writings have influenced Masonic practices for 150 years. Pike served as a Confederate general during the War and is the only Confederate soldier to have a statue in Washington, D.C., at Judiciary Square.

From its beginning in Charleston, the Scottish Rite has spread throughout the world. Currently there are around 170,000 Scottish Rite Masons, with about 4000 of them attaining the Thirty-third degree. All regular Supreme Councils of the world today descended from the Charleston Lodge.

25 1801 FIRST COUPLE TO HONEYMOON AT NIAGARA FALLS

Aaron Burr spent the summer of 1800 at his New York estate, Richmond Hill, preparing for the national elections as the Democratic-Republican vice-presidential candidate. During that time, his daughter Theodosia acquired a serious suitor, South Carolina planter Joseph Alston, who was vacationing in the area.

Alston accompanied Burr in a trip through New England to solidify support for the coming fall election. The two men became close friends, with Alston serving as Burr's voice in the South for the Republicans.

In the presidential election Burr and Thomas Jefferson received the same number of electoral votes. The election was so close that it was thrown into the United States House of Representatives who chose Jefferson as president and Burr as vice-president.

On February 2, 1801, Theodosia Burr married Joseph Alston. It was speculated that there was more than romance involved in their union. Robert Troup, one of Burr's best friends wrote that:

> the marriage was an affair of Burr, not of his daughter, and that the money in question was the predominant motive.

Aaron Burr agonized about money matters, particularly as to how he would hold on to the Richmond Hill (NY) estate. His daughter's marriage to a member of the Southern gentry helped relieve him of his financial burdens. The marriage also meant that Theodosia would become prominent in South Carolina social circles.

Not everyone was supportive of the marriage. Hannah Gallatin, wife of Jefferson's secretary of state wrote:

> Reports do not speak well of him [Alston]: it says he is rich, but he is a great dasher, dissipated, ill-tempered, vain and silly. I know that he is ugly and of unprepossessing manners. Can it be that the father had sacrificed a daughter to affluence and influential connections?

Despite all this negativity, it was Theodosia who had chosen Alston, and their correspondence indicates it was a relationship of mutual love and admiration.

During their wedding trip they stayed at Niagara Falls, the first recorded honeymoon couple to do so.

In 1802 their son, Aaron Burr Alston, was born in Charleston. At the time, Joseph Alson owned the house at 94 Church Street. Two years later, in the most famous duel in American history, Vice President Burr killed Alexander Hamilton in New Jersey. During the initial outcry against Burr, the vice-president fled to South Carolina, spending time in Charleston and a low country plantation.

Joseph Alston was elected governor of South Carolina in 1812 and soon after his son died. The ill and heart-broken Theodosia left South Carolina to visit her father in New York. Her ship was lost at sea several days later.

26 1823   FIRST PUBLIC FIREPROOF BUILDING CONSTRUCTED IN AMERICA

The first fireproof building in the United States was designed by Robert Mills and constructed in Charleston as a repository for public documents, at a cost of $56,000. During his long career as an architect and engineer, Robert Mills spread his legacy across the United States.

Robert Mills was born in Charlestown on August 12, 1781, during the British occupation. His father was a tailor, respectable, successful but solidly middle class. Mills is often erroneously referred to as America's first native-born architect, but Charles Bullfinch of Boston has a clearer claim to that honor.

James Hoban, a Philadelphia-based architect spent 1787-1792 in South Carolina. During his time in Charleston Hoban conducted an "evening school, for the instruction of young men in Architecture." It is often speculated that Mills attended these classes, but there is no documentation of that fact. If not, based on the quality of his earliest drawings (1802), Mills must have attended similar classes offered to young men in Charleston. Newspapers at the time advertised that M. Depresseville:

> Continues to keep his Drawing School, in different Part of Landscapes, with Pencil or Washed, teaches Architecture, and to draw with method; also the necessary acknowledgements for the Plans.

Another advertisement claimed that Thomas Walker, a stone cutter and mason from Edinburgh:

opened an evening school for teaching the rules of
Architecture from seven to nine in the evening (four
nights a week)

In 1800, at age nineteen, Mills moved to Washington, D.C. and
was hired by James Hoban. The Irish architect had won the design
competition of the President's House (the White House). In
December 1800 Mills was "pursuing studies in the office of the
architect of the President's House."

Under Hoban, who was also supervising the construction of the
Capital, Mills served as an apprentice/assistant. He spent most of his
time drawing wainscot, staircases and doorways. He learned the
most rudimentary skills of construction – labor and material
management. During the next two years Mills in Washington,
gained exposure to a variety of architectural styles as the new capital
city was rapidly expanded.

President Thomas Jefferson befriended Mills during this time
and "offered me the use of his library." Jefferson also wanted
drawings of his home, Monticello, and he "engaged Mr. Mills to
make out drawings of the general plan and elevation of the building."

In 1802, Mills submitted designs for the proposed South Carolina
College and won the $300 prize, but none of his designs were ever
used. He then spent eight years working for Benjamin Latrobe,
Surveyor of Public Buildings, a Jefferson appointee.

Mills wrote that Latrobe was:

Engaged upon the Delaware and Chesapeake Canal and
as an architect of the Capitol at Washington, at which
time I entered his office as a student under the advice
and recommendation of Mr. Jefferson, then President of
the United States.

Latrobe later described Mills as possessing:

that valuable substitute for genius - laborious precision –
in a very high degree, and is therefore very useful to me,
though his professional education has been hitherfor
much misdirected.

Ruins of the Circular Congregational Church, Charleston, circa 1880s.
Photograph shows the damage from the 1861 fire that ravaged the city.
Courtesy Library of Congress.

During this time Mills also submitted plans for two Charleston churches, an alteration of St. Michael's (never implemented) and a design for the Congregational Church. Dr. David Ramsay presented the idea of a round church in 1803 saying his "wife suggested the idea and sketched a plan." In February 1804 the church building committee thanked Mills:

> for his ingenious and elegant drawings which had essentially assisted the Members and Supporters in forming a correct opinion of the form and plan of their proposed building.

Mills's plans called for a rotunda eighty-eight-feet in diameter and thirty-three-feet-high, covered by a hemispherical Delorme made of wood and sheathed in copper, capped by a large cupola. His church design was drastically altered when the building was constructed in 1806, much to Mills's displeasure.

In 1819 South Carolina established an Internal Improvements Program for the creation of canals, roads and public buildings. With a budget of $1 million spread over ten years, it was per capita the largest public-works-improvement project of any state in America. Mills was hired as Acting Commissioner for Public Buildings with his main task to design (or redesign) courthouses and jails across the state. In addition, the state legislature had noted the need for fireproof buildings as records repositories throughout the state and appropriated $50,000 for the design and construction.

On May 20, 1822, Charleston City Council voted to pay Mills $200 to design a fireproof building on the square behind City Hall, to be used for county records. Mills envisioned the building as part of a public square which embraced the park (later named Washington Square), City Hall, the County Courthouse and a proposed-federal courthouse.

Fireproof Building, Charleston. *Courtesy Library of Congress*

In December 1823 Mills lost his position as Superintendent of Public Buildings but was appointed as one of four "Commissioners for completing Fire Proof Buildings." He was also appointed Commissioner of Public Buildings for Charleston District, even though he was living in the state capital, Columbia.

Throughout 1825-26, under the supervision of contractor John Spindle, the construction of the Fireproof Building proceeded. All materials were non-flammable – granite, brownstone, flagstone, brick, metal and copper. On December 11, 1826, it was finished and "ready for occupancy." The final cost of the project was $53,803.81.

In 1836 Robert Mills won a private design competition conducted by the Washington National Monument Committee for the construction of a permanent memorial to George Washington in the nation's capital. His original design called for a 600-foot-tall square shaft rising from a Greco-Roman circular colonnade, supported by thirty Doric columns, 45-feet high and 12-feet in diameter.

By the time the cornerstone was laid July 4, 1848, the memorial design had been scaled back to a more stream-lined, elegant structure, now one of the most famous landmarks in the United States.

Mills died on March 3, 1855 with more than 50 projects to his credit, which include more than thirty county courthouses and jail buildings in South Carolina.

A list of Robert Mills's most important projects include:

1804

- Circular Congregational Church, Charleston, S.C.

1806

- South Carolina Penitentiary, Columbia, S.C.

1809

- Franklin Row, Philadelphia, Pa
- State House (Independence Hall) Wings, Philadelphia, Pa.

1812

- First Unitarian (Octagon) Church, Philadelphia, Pa

1813

- Washington Monument, Baltimore, Md.

1816

- Winchester Monument, Baltimore, Md.
- First Baptist Church, Baltimore, Md.

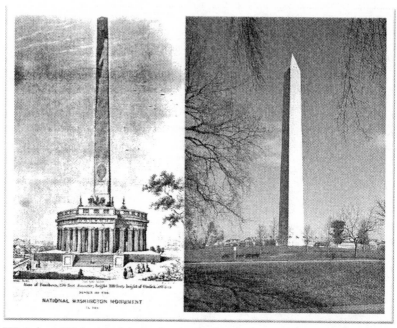

LEFT: Robert Mills' original design for the Washington Monument. Courtesy *National Archives*. RIGHT: Washington Monument completed. *Courtesy Library of Congress.*

1817

- St. John's Episcopal Church, Baltimore, Md.

1818

- First Baptist Church, Charleston S.C.

1821

- Colleton County Courthouse; Colleton County Jail, Walterboro, S.C.
- Columbia Canal, Columbia, S.C.

1822

- Charleston County Jail (addition), Charleston, S.C.

- County Records Office – Fireproof Building, Charleston, S.C.
- Powder Magazine Complex, Charleston, S.C.
- South Carolina Asylum, Columbia, S.C

1823

- Horry County Courthouse and Jail, Conway, S.C.
- Union County Courthouse, Union, S.C.

1824

- St. Peter's Church, Columbia, S.C.
- Maxcy Monument, Columbia, S.C.

1825

- *Atlas of the State of South Carolina*
- Edgefield County Courthouse, Edgefield, S.C.

1826

- Elevated railroad, Washington, D.C. to New Orleans
- Newberry County Jail, Newberry, S.C.

1830

- U.S. Senate (renovation), Washington, D.C.

1831

- Marine Hospital, Charleston, S.C.
- Washington Canal, Washington, D.C.

1832

- Executive Offices and White House (water systems), Washington, D.C.
- House of Representatives (alterations), Washington, D.C.

1833

- Customs House, New London, Ct.
- Customs House, New Bedford, Ma.

1834

- U.S. Capital (water system), Washington, D.C.

1836

- U.S. Patent Office, Washington, D.C.
- South Caroliniana Library, Columbia, S.C.
- U.S. Treasury Building, Washington, D.C.

1839

- Library and Science Building, U.S. Military Academy, West Point, N.Y.
- U.S. Post Office, Washington, D.C.

1845

- Washington National Monument, Washington, D.C.

1847

- Smithsonian Institution (supervising architect), Washington, D.C.

1852

- University of Virginia Library (addition, renovation), Charlottesville, Va.

27 182 FIRST REFORMED SOCIETY OF ISRAELITES IN AMERICA

Kahal Kadosh Beth Elohm (Holy Congregation of God) was organized in 1749 in Charleston, making it the fourth oldest Jewish congregation in the United States. Prayers were originally recited in private homes but in 1775 an improvised synagogue was built, adjacent to the present-day location on Hasell Street.

In 1792 a Georgian style, cupolated synagogue was built, considered the "largest and most impressive." In America. When Lafayette visited Charleston in 1825, a member of his entourage described it "spacious and elegant." Unfortunately, that structure was destroyed by the great fire in 1838. Two years later, the current Greek Revival structure was built.

On December 23, 1824, forty-seven members, led by Isaac Harby and Abraham Moise, petitioned the Adjunta (trustees) to change the Sephardic Orthodox liturgy, noting they had "witnessed with deep regret, the apathy and neglect which have been manifested towards our holy religion."

The petition asked for an abridgement of the Hebrew ritual, English translation of the prayers and a sermon delivered in English. It was denied.

On January 16 these members "withdrew from the congregation, and joining a larger number who were not members, establishing a new place of worship." They called themselves "The Reformed Society of Israelites." They met at Seyle's Masonic Hall at 209 Meeting Street.

For the next nine years the "Reformed Society" and Beth Elohim met separately. Then Beth Elohim adopted many of the reformed practices and principles. Today, the actions of the Reformed Society of Israelites are acknowledged at the birth of Reform Judaism in the United States.

In 1873 Beth Elohim became one of the founding synagogues of the Union of American Hebrew Congregations.

Kahal Kodosh Beth Elohim, 90 Hasell Street, Charleston, 1840.
Courtesy Library of Congress

28 1828   POINSETTIA PLANT INTRODUCED TO AMERICA

During the Christmas season, households throughout the world are decorated with blinking lights, trees, candles and bright red plants – poinsettias. In 2014 more than 40 million were sold in America, making it the country's best-selling potted plant.

The Aztecs called the plant "Cuetlaxachitl" and used the sap to control fevers. The leaves were used to make a reddish dye. The Aztecs considered red to be a symbol of purity, so poinsettias were traditionally part of their religious ceremonies. Montezuma, last of the Aztec kings, brought the plant into what is now Mexico City. In Mexico and Guatemala, the poinsettia is called the "Flower of the Holy Night" referring to Christmas Eve.

The official botanical name, *Euphorbia pulcherrima*, was assigned by German botanist Karl Ludwig Wilenow in 1833. The plant grew though a crack in his greenhouse, and, dazzled by its color he gave it the botanical name which roughly means "very beautiful."

So where does the name "poinsettia" come from? A native Charlestonian, of course, Joel Roberts Poinsett.

Poinsett was born in Charleston on March 2, 1779, son of a prominent physician. After his education in New England and Europe he returned to Charleston, hoping to pursue a military career. His father, however, disapproved. Hoping to entice his son to settle into the local aristocracy, Dr. Poinsett arranged for him to study law under Henry William DeSaussure.

Within a year, however, Joel became bored with his law studies and in 1801 moved to France to travel the Continent, He scaled Mount Etna on the island of Sicily and then hiked through the Alps into Switzerland. Blessed with a quick and curious mind, Poinsett was always interested in the varieties of plants he encountered in his journeys, becoming an avid amateur botanist.

Poinsett returned to Charleston in January 1804 to deal with family matters. His father had died several months earlier and his sister, Susan, was in poor health and she also soon died. As the sole remaining heir, Poinsett was bequeathed a small fortune, including town houses and city lots, plantations, bank stock and "English funds." The entire Poinsett estate was valued at a more than $100,000. Settling his affairs, he decided to resume his travels.

Joel Roberts Poinsett. *Courtesy Library of Congress*

Poinsett arrived in the Russian capital of St. Petersburg in November 1806 and was introduced to the Russian court by Levit Harris, U.S. consul. Learning that Poinsett was from South Carolina, the Dowager Empress Maria Feodorovna asked him to inspect the cotton factories under her patronage. Poinsett and Harris traveled by sleigh to Cronstadt where, after inspections, Poinsett recommended several improvements. He also assessed that the cotton industry would never be successful in Russia because serfs received no compensation and therefore would have no interest in its success. He believed that the institution of serfdom made it difficult for Russia to ever become industrialized, an odd opinion for a man who had grown up surrounded by the pervasive institution of slavery.

Poinsett dined at the Palace with Czar Alexander who attempted to entice him into the Russian civil or military service. Poinsett was hesitant, which prompted Alexander to advise him to "see the Empire, acquire the language, study the people," before making his decision. For the next several months, Poinsett traveled to southern Russia, after which he was offered the rank of colonel in the Russian army.

Poinsett, however, was eager to return to the United States. News arrived that the U.S.S *Chesapeake* had been attacked by a British warship, and there was the distinct prospect of a new war with Great Britain.

Upon his return to America Poinsett was appointed Consul-General by President James Madison. He was dispatched to South American to assess the revolutionary movements in Chile and Argentina, in their struggle for independence from Spain.

After serving in the House of Representatives, on June 1, 1825, President John Quincy Adams appointed Poinsett the first United States minister to Mexico.

Poinsett became friends with the Spanish minister to Mexico, Don Angel Calderon de la Barca. During his stay he often wandered the Mexican countryside, looking for new plant species. In 1828 he visited the area south of Mexico City around Taxco del Alarcon, where he found a beautiful shrub growing along the roadside, which the locals called "Flor de Noche Buena" (Christmas Eve flower). Poinsett sent samples home to his plantations in Charleston and Greenville, South Carolina.

Most botanists dismissed the plant as nothing more than a weed, but Poinsett shared it with friends and other horticulturists whose enthusiasm for its beauty was tempered only by its short bloom time. Initially Americans called it "painted leaf" or the "Mexican fire plant."

Two of the plant recipients were John Bartram, Jr. of Philadelphia, whose family had established one of the first plant nurseries in America, and Robert Buist, also from Pennsylvania.

In 1836, when Spanish Minister de la Barca was in Washington, D.C., he took great interest in a new book being written by William Hickling Prescott, titled *History of the Reign of Ferdinand and Isabella.* Prescott, a botanist and historian, was also the author of the just-published *Conquest of Mexico*, part of which detailed Poinsett's adventures in Mexico. De la Barca asked Prescott if he might be able to come up with a less scientific, more pleasing name for Poinsett's "Mexican fire plant."

Following the 19th-century convention of naming things after their "discoverers," Prescott suggested calling it the "poinsettia."

In March 1837, Poinsett was appointed as secretary of war by President Martin Van Buren. During his time as secretary he presided over the continuing removal of Indians from the east to areas west of the Mississippi River and the Second Seminole War in Florida.

In his later life, Poinsett became a founding member of the National Institute for the Promotion of Science and the Useful, later was renamed the Smithsonian Institute.

Poinsett died December 12, 1852. One-hundred-and-fifty years later, in 2002, the House of Representatives created Poinsettia Day, to honor Joel Poinsett, and passed a resolution to honor Paul Ecke Jr., as the father of the poinsettia industry.

The Ecke family started in business in 1909 with a fruit and vegetable stand on Sunset Blvd. in Los Angeles. Poinsettias grew wild in the area and the family began to sell the cut flowers. In 1915 the Ecke family purchased five acres to grow poinsettias and within two years were shipping the plants all across America.

Paul Ecke Jr. marketed poinsettias to Hollywood, providing free plants to decorate the sets of TV shows, such as *The Tonight Show*, *The Dinah Shore Show* and *Bob Hope's Christmas Specials*. He also convinced woman's magazines like *The Ladies Home Journal* and *Better Homes & Gardens* to feature poinsettias, especially in the December issues.

Through Ecke's ingenious and tireless marketing, the poinsettia has become the number one selling potted plant in America, and is as ubiquitous with Christmas eve as reindeer and Santa Claus.

29 1830 FIRST REGULARLY-SCHEDULED PASSENGER TRAIN SERVICE IN AMERICA

The Charleston & Hamburg Rail Road (C&HRR) was chartered by Alexander Black and William Aiken on December 19, 1827. Black proposed to build and operate a "railed road" from Charleston to Hamburg, Columbia and Camden. Stock was offered at $100 a share with the goal of raising $700,000 to finance the building of the railroad.

Charleston's economy heavily depended on the shipment of three staples: cotton to England, rice to southern Europe and lumber to the West Indies. The development of small steamers that sailed the upper Savannah River had negatively impacted trade in Charleston harbor. These small ships sailed north and brought crops from Georgia and South Carolina downriver to Augusta, Georgia, where the cargo was loaded on larger vessels and taken to Savannah, bypassing Charleston.

The proposed railroad from Hamburg, located on the Savannah River across from Augusta, was considered the best economic solution. The commodities could be transported by rail 136 miles from Augusta to Charleston.

On May 17, 1828, Horatio Allen, chief engineer of the Delaware & Hudson Canal Company, met with officials of C&HRR. They discussed the type of railroad to build and Allan recommended using a steam locomotive. He had studied them in England and was positive that these steam engines were the wave of the future.

In January 1829 construction of the C&HRR began on the Charleston outskirts at Line Street, as the railroad was not permitted to operate within the city limits. Chief engineer Horatio Allen decided the track gauge (width between the two rails) should be five feet rather than the proposed four and a half, for greater stability.

The first experimental run was conducted on March 20, 1830, by a four-wheeled wind-powered cart. Equipped with a sail this cart "sailed" along from Line Street for less than a mile. The *Charleston Courier* reported that:

> Fifteen gentlemen got on board and flew off at the rate of 12 to 15 miles an hour ... The mast went by the board with the sail and rigging attached, carrying with them several of the crew.

The construction of a steam-engine locomotive for the Charleston & Hamburg Rail Road was begun during the summer at West Point Foundry in Cold Spring, N.Y. A Charleston businessman E. L. Miller provided $4000 for its construction. When it was tested at West Point, it was reported that:

> the *Best Friend* was a four wheel engine ... two inclined cylinders ... working down on a double crank, inside of the frame, with the wheels outside the frame, each wheel connecting together outside, with outside rods. The wheels were iron hub, wooden spokes ... with iron tire ...the whole machine weighed four and a half tons.

On October 23, the unassembled *Best Friend* arrived in Charleston on the freighter *Niagra*. It was taken to the shop of Thomas Dotter and reassembled. By the end of November, five miles of railroad track had been laid from Line Street to San Souci, a small community north of Charleston. Two weeks later, December 14, the *Best Friend* locomotive pulled two fourteen-foot coaches with forty men on board at a speed of twenty miles per hour.

On Christmas Eve, the *Charleston Courier* reported:

> The public are respectfully informed that the Rail Road Company has purchased from Mr. E.L. Miller his locomotive steam engine and that it will hereafter be constantly employed in the transportation of passengers. The time of leaving the station in Line Street will be 8 o'clock, at 10 A.M. at 1 and half past

three o'clock P.M. Great punctuality will be observed in the time of starting.

The *Best Friend* locomotive. *Author's Collection.*

At 8:00 A.M. on Christmas day, the first regularly scheduled passenger train in America pulled away from the Line Street station. Nicholas W. Darrell operated the locomotive as engineer for the 10-mile round trip between Charleston and San Souci. The trip was described by a writer, Jockey of York:

> Away we flew on the wings of the wind as the speed of 15 to 25 miles per hour, annihilating time and space ... leaving all the world behind. It was nine minutes, five and one-fourth seconds since we started and we have discovered ourselves beyond the forks of the State and Dorchester Roads ... We came to San Souci in quick time. Here we stopped to take up a recruiting party, darted forth like a live rocket, scattering sparks and flames on either side, passed over three saltwater creeks, hop, step and jump and landed us all at the

> Lines before any of us had time to determine where or
> not it was prudent to be scared.

More than 140 passengers made the first trip, riding in two cars. During the first day, the *Best Friend* carried more than 500 passengers. Truly, it was one of the most wondrous Christmases in Charleston history.

Within five months a second locomotive, the *West Point*, was put into operation and track laying operations continued. Three years later the railroad from Charleston to Hamburg was complete, 136 miles – the longest railroad in the world at the time. The cost of the project was $950,000. The next day, a special "dignitaries" train ran from Charleston to Aiken, South Carolina, with Governor Robert Y. Hayne on board.

Until that moment, travel had been limited by road conditions and river navigability. The railroad overcame all these obstacles and provided a much-needed boost to the Lowcountry. At one point, there were six locomotives in operation on the Charleston & Hamburg line.

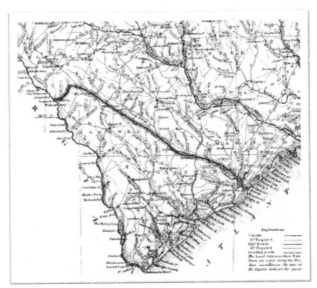

Route of the Charleston & Hamburg Rail Road. *Author's collection.*

30 1831 FIRST FATALITY ON AN AMERICAN RAILROAD

On June 17, the *Best Friend* boiler exploded while picking up lumber cars at the "forks in the road," where Dorchester and State roads merged, near the Eight Mile House. Engineer Nicholas Darrell wrote:

> When I ran the *Best Friend*, I had a Negro fireman to fire, clean and grease the engine. This Negro, annoyed at the noise occasioned by the blowing off the steam, fastened the valve-lever down and sat upon it which caused the explosion, badly injuring him.

This nameless black fireman, who died from his injuries, was the first fatality on an American railroad. The explosion ended all train service on the Charleston and Hamburg Rail Road for a month. Part of the *Best Friend* wreckage was later used to cast a cannon for the Confederate army.

31 1832 FIRST CHILDREN'S NEWSPAPER PUBLISHED IN AMERICA

Caroline Howard was born in Boston on October 1, 1794. She would eventually become famous for pushing the boundaries of a woman's place in 19th-century society, while espousing the traditional woman's role in her writing. Her "domestic" novels encouraged women to find satisfaction in their "domestic duties" all while her own were being carried out by slaves in her fashionable Charleston home.

With both of her parents dead by the time she was four, Caroline was raised by her older sister in Boston. She developed an interest in literature at an early age, writing poetry but adhering to the social standard of the day that "publishing was unladylike."

She spent her summers in Georgia with her brother, introducing Caroline to the more mannerly, sedate lifestyle of southern ladies and gentlemen. At age sixteen, one of her poems, "Jephthah's Rash Vow" was published in her school newspaper without her consent which distressed her. She wrote that she was "as alarmed as if I had been detected in men's apparel!"

That same year she met Samuel Gilman, a student at Harvard and a fellow poet. According to her biography their first meeting was "a pretty bit of romance." She had gone to Cambridge for a social event at which Samuel was present. In a game of forfeits he found himself called upon to recite a bit of poetry and gave the opening lines of "Jephthah's Rash Vow:"

> The battle had ceased, and the victory was won,
> The wild cry of horror was o'er:
> Now rose in his glory the bright beaming sun,
> And with him, his journey the war-chief begun,

With a soul breathing vengeance no more.

Gilman was unaware that the poem's author was in attendance. This was the beginning of their courtship.

Caroline Gilman, from *Cyclopaedia of American Literature*, 1855.
Author's collection

They were married in Georgia on September 25, 1819, and moved to Charleston where Samuel served as minister of the Unitarian Church. They quickly became important figures in Charleston's social and literary circles. Samuel supported his wife's literary aspirations but expected her to fulfill her traditional role as a minister's wife. He had reservations about women who "chose to move on the agitating theatre of public life." He felt her role was to "impress among the tender minds of youth the precepts of religion."

After the birth of their first child in 1831, Caroline founded *The Rose Bud*, the first weekly magazine for juveniles. She produced most of the literary content herself, including three serialized novels, dozens of stories and thousands of poems.

RECOLLECTIONS

OF A

SOUTHERN MATRON.

BY CAROLINE GILMAN,

AUTHOR OF

"RECOLLECTIONS OF A NEW ENGLAND HOUSEKEEPER."

" Me thinketh it accordant to reson
To tellen you alle the condition
Of eche of hem, so as it seemed to me ;
And whiche they weren ; and of what degre ;
And eke in what avail that they were inne ;
And at a knight, then wol I firste beginne."
CHAUCER.

NEW-YORK:

HARPER & BROTHERS, 82 CLIFF-STREET.

1838.

Title page of Caroline Gilman's *Recollections of A Southern Matron*, 1838, *Author's collection*

In 1834 she published the popular *Recollections of a New England Housekeeper*, a novel about an attorney's wife who trains country women to be house servants. Four years later she published another popular novel, *Recollections of a Southern Matron*, the story of a young girl raised on a plantation, which attempted to illustrate the similarities between northern and southern households. She also edited the *Boston Lady's Annual Register* and also the *Housewife's Memorandum-Book*.

All this made her the most famous female writer in the South, mainly because she continued to espouse the tradition feminine role in society. Her writing always emphasized the natural hierarchy in the male-female relationship using the constant theme that the preservation of family harmony was a woman's most important duty and

However, it was Caroline's support of another hierarchy, namely slavery, which began to alienate most of her northern readers. She called slavery "the strength and almost the very life-blood of this Southern Region." As the abolition movement grew more prominent in the North, her popularity there waned.

In January 1840 Caroline wrote to her sister and complained that she had developed "something amounting to aversion to the whole writing process [which] seemed to be almost a disease."

In 1848, in a brief autobiography, she wrote:

> I find myself, then, at nearly sixty years of age, somewhat of a patriarch in the line of American female authors—a kind of Past Master in the order.

Following Samuel's death in February 1858, Caroline remained in South Carolina. During the Civil War, she publicly supported the southern cause to the end. She outlived all but one of her children and died on September 15, 1888, at the age of 94.

Samuel and Caroline Gilman marker at the Unitarian graveyard, Charleston.
Photo by author.

32 1837 FIRST MUNICIPAL COLLEGE IN AMERICA

On January 30, 1770, Lt. Governor William Bull (see #5) recommended to the General Assembly the "establishment of a provincial college." However, due to financial concerns, political rivalries and the disruption of the American Revolution, the idea was never acted upon.

On March 19, 1785, the General Assembly granted a charter for the College of Charleston to "encourage and institute youth in the several branches of liberal education." The founders of the College included three signers of the Declaration of Independence - Edward Rutledge, Arthur Middleton and Thomas Heyward - and three future signers of the United States Constitution - John Rutledge, Charles Pinckney and Charles Cotesworth Pinckney.

In 1791 the trustees hired Reverend Robert Smith as the first president of the college. Smith held classes at his home on Glebe Street, which is currently the President's House on the college campus.

Rev. Smith was educated in England and served as rector of St. Philip's Church during the American Revolution. He supported the Patriot cause and even served as a soldier during the British siege of Charlestown in 1780. While serving as president of the college, Smith became the first Episcopal bishop of South Carolina and re-located the college from his house one block north, to a brick barracks that had quartered soldiers during the War, near a water cistern, called Cistern Yard.

In 1794 the college graduated its first class of six students, the oldest being eighteen-years-old. The academic work for the degree was so easy that one of the graduates said "the whole thing was absurd."

The Bishop's House (Robert Smith House) at 6 Glebe Street, where the first classes of the College of Charleston were held. *Courtesy Library of Congress.*

Rev. Smith resigned as president in 1797. The college held classes only intermittently, eventually closing in 1811. Thirteen years later, in 1824, the trustees hired Rev. Jasper Adams from Brown University as its new president. Adams's main accomplishment was the construction of the first building on Cistern Yard, later named Randolph Hall. However, most of his plans for the school were opposed by the General Assembly because it was contrary to the interests of a pet legislative project - South Carolina College in Columbia (the University of South Carolina).

Two years later Rev. Adams left in frustration and the future of the college seemed in doubt. In 1837 the city of Charleston declared that "it would be in the city's interest to have a home college" and took control of the school, assuming its financial responsibilities.

This action made the College of Charleston America's first municipal college.

In 1850 the city provided financing for the expansion of the main academic building, the future Randolph Hall, and for the construction of Porters Lodge. They also allocated money to enclose the Cistern Yard with a fence, the block that is currently the main campus.

College of Charleston, Cistern Yard with Randolph Hall.
Courtesy Library of Congress.

During the Civil War most of the students and faculty left to serve the Confederacy. Classes resumed on February 1, 1866, and for the next ninety years the college persevered. Under the leadership of President Harrison Randolph (1897-1945) women were admitted. Enrollment increased from sixty-eight students in 1905 to more than 400 in 1935.

In the 1950s the college became a private institution in an attempt to avoid racial integration. The first black students finally were enrolled in 1967.

In 1970 the College of Charleston became a state institution, with an enrollment of 500. Today it boasts an enrollment of more than 11,000 undergraduates, with six academic schools.

Notable people who have attended the College include:

- JOHN CHARLES FRÉMONT: the Great Pathfinder. Fremont explored the West as a scout for the U.S. Army in the 1830s and 1840s and served as governor of California. In 1856 Fremont was the first Republican nominee for president. During the Civil War, he served as a major general in the Union army.
- VINCENT DI PASQUALE: music producer and remixer who has had hits with Lauryn Hill, Nelly Furtado and Mariah Carey. His remix of Madonna's "4 Minutes" went to No. 1 on *Billboard's* hot dance/club play chart.
- THOMAS GIBSON: actor, *Dharma & Greg; Chicago Hope; Criminal Minds*
- ANTHONY JOHNSON: NBA player
- ORLANDO JONES: actor, *MADtv; Office Space; Sleepy Hollow.*
- NAFEES BIN ZAFAR: 2007 Academy Award winner for the development of fluid simulation software used in film; Principle Engineer at DreamWorks Animation. Worked on movies including: *Pirates of the Caribbean: At World's End; Shrek Forever; 2012; Puss in Boots.*
- CARY ANN HEARST: singer/songwriter, member of the Americana band, Shovels & Rope.

33 1860   FIRST STATE TO SECEDE FROM THE UNION

December 20, 1860. 1:15 P.M.

South Carolina seceded from the Union. Rev. A. Toomer Porter, an Episcopal priest from Charleston wrote in his autobiography:

> The ordinance of secession was read, and a stillness that could be felt prevailed ... Yea after yea, was answered until every name was called and the vote was unanimous.

The delegates also voted to form the Republic of South Carolina. Like most important events in history, South Carolina's secession did not happen in a vacuum. There were thirty years of contentious issues that slowly, gradually pulled South Carolina out of the United States.

The state leaders had a well-established history of rebellious attitude and contentious behavior. They had been instrumental in two revolutions during the first 160 years of South Carolina's history – the overthrow of the Lords Proprietors in 1719; the establishment of the Republic of South Carolina in 1776; and the bloodiest fight for independence from Great Britain during the American Revolution.

The Missouri Compromise of 1820 was Congress's first kick-the-can-down-the-road effort in dealing with the issue of slavery, since the Constitutional Convention of 1787. Missouri requested admission as a slave state. At the time, there were twenty-two states in the Union, evenly divided between free and slave.

To keep the balance and the peace, Congress admitted Missouri as a slave state and Maine as free. It also passed a bill that drew a line across the former Louisiana Territory, establishing a boundary between free and slave states.

Like most compromises, no one was happy with the result. People from the North argued that it made the federal government complicit in the extension of slavery. Southern politicians criticized the law because it established the principle that Congress could make laws regarding slavery, previously viewed strictly as a state's right.

The argument was just beginning.

In 1828 Congress passed what became known as the "Tariff of Abominations." It protected industries in the North by placing a tariff on imported goods. This forced people in the South to pay higher prices for them. Vice President John C. Calhoun of South Carolina argued that the tariff was unconstitutional, because it favored manufacturing over commerce and agriculture.

Calhoun anonymously wrote a pamphlet in December 1828 titled *The South Carolina Exposition and Protest* which urged the tariff nullification in South Carolina. When Andrew Jackson's administration failed to address South Carolina's complaints, the Nullification movement began to grow. Over the next few years, the passion for secession and states' rights smoldered.

On July 14, 1832, President Jackson signed the Tariff of 1832 which made some rate reductions, but for South Carolina it was too little too late. In November a state convention met and adopted an Ordinance of Nullification, which declared the tariffs of 1828 and 1832 "unconstitutional and unenforceable in South Carolina." Any federal attempt to use force in collecting the taxes would lead South Carolina to secede.

On December 12 the South Carolina Assembly elected Calhoun to the U.S. Senate and on December 28, 1832 he resigned the vice-presidency. In his new position, Calhoun hoped he could more forcefully continue the Nullification fight.

President Jackson pushed the Force Bill through Congress, giving him the power to close any American port at his discretion. The president then wrote to the people of South Carolina:

> Seduced as you may have been, my fellow countrymen
> by the theories and misrepresentation of ambitious,
> deluded & designing men ... the first act of resistance to
> the laws which have been denounced as void ... is
> Treason. Can you consent to become Traitors?

In a blatant challenge to the president of the United States, the South Carolina legislature nullified the Force Bill. Jackson threatened to send U.S. Navy ships to Charleston to enforce the tariff. In response to President Jackson, a group of Charleston men planned to meet one night, board a New York ship in Charleston harbor and toss its cargo overboard, a Southern reenactment of the Boston Tea party. But cooler heads prevailed and a political compromise between Henry Clay and Calhoun averted any further confrontation.

However, the entire episode left South Carolina political leaders wary of the ever-powerful federal government. Robert Barnwell Rhett, a state senator, summed up the Nullification Crisis with the warning:

> Let Gentlemen not be deceived ... until this Government
> is made a limited Government ... there is no liberty – no
> security for the South.

On July 29, 1835, Charleston Postmaster Alfred Huger discovered antislavery pamphlets in the mailbags delivered overnight from the North. Huger considered the material a call for black revolution. He locked up the pamphlets until President Jackson could send instructions on their dispensation. Word quickly spread throughout the city.

South Carolina leaders were adamant that abolitionist ideas should not be allowed to enter public discussion. That night a mob of "respectable" slave owners raided the Charleston post office. The event was described in a local newspaper:

> The pamphlets were burned by 8 p.m. the next evening
> opposite the main guard house, 3000 persons being
> present. The effigies of Arthur Tappan, Dr. Cox and W.L.
> Garrison were at the same time suspended. A 9 o'clock
> a balloon was let off, and the effigies were consumed
> by the neck, with the offensive documents at their feet.

Eleven years later, in 1846, Congressman David Wilmot of Pennsylvania introduced a bill to ban slavery in any territory acquired from Mexico. The Wilmot Proviso was blocked by the southern-dominated Senate. However, it inflamed the growing controversy over slavery, and helped bring about the formation of the Republican Party.

During the first week of June 1850, more than 150 delegates from Virginia, South Carolina, Georgia, Alabama, Mississippi, Texas, Arkansas, Florida and Tennessee met at McKendree Methodist Church in Nashville to consider a possible course of action if Congress decided to exclude slavery in the new territories.

On March 20, 1852, *Uncle Tom's Cabin* was published. Written by Harriet Beecher Stowe, it had originally been released to a limited audience as a forty-week serial in an abolitionist periodical, *The National Era*. As a book *Uncle Tom's Cabin* became a runaway best-seller, with more than 10,000 copies sold during its first week. It its first year, the book sold more than 2 million copies in the United States and Great Britain. It forever changed how many Americans viewed slavery.

The book, of course, was decried across the South. It was called "criminal and slanderous." South Carolina novelist William Gilmore Simms, declared *Uncle Tom's Cabin* to be "utterly false." He quickly wrote *The Sword and the Distaff*, a refutation of Stowe's work.

The Kansas-Nebraska Act of 1854 created new territories which opened up thousands of acres for settlement and made a transcontinental railroad economically feasible. It also had the unintended consequence of repealing the 1820 Missouri Compromise. Congress inserted popular sovereignty into the Act which allowed white male settlers in each territory to vote whether to enter the Union as a free or slave state. Both proslavery and antislavery settlers flooded into Kansas in hopes of tipping the balance of power in their favor.

In December 1855, more than one-thousand Missourians crossed the border into Lawrence, Kansas, a free-state stronghold. On May 21, 1856, anti-slavery supporters looted the town. In response, fiery abolitionist John Brown organized the murder of five proslavery settlers along Pottawatomie Creek. These murders unleashed four months of violence as small armies clashed all over

Kansas. Horace Greeley, of the *New York Tribune*, labeled the events "Bleeding Kansas." Calm and reasoned debate over the slavery issue was no longer possible.

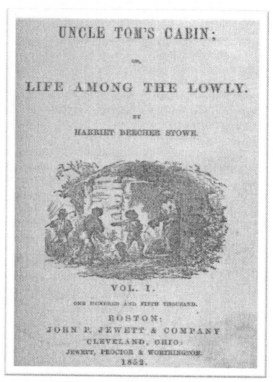

First edition *Uncle Tom's Cabin*, 1852. *Courtesy Library of Congress*

Senator Charles Sumner, a Republican from Massachusetts, gave a speech on the Senate floor against slavery, called "The Crime Against Kansas." He railed against the:

> murderous robbers from Missouri ... hirelings, picked from the drunken spew and vomit of an uneasy civilization.

During his two-day tirade, he specifically singled out Democrat U.S. Senator Andrew Butler of South Carolina for criticism. At one point he called him an "imbecile."

The senator from South Carolina has read many books of chivalry, and believes himself a chivalrous knight with sentiments of honor and courage. Of course he has chosen a mistress to whom he has made his vows, and who, though ugly to others, is always lovely to him; though polluted in the sight of the world, is chaste in his sight -- I mean the harlot, slavery. For her his tongue is always profuse in words. Let her be impeached in character, or any proposition made to shut her out from the extension of her wantonness, and no extravagance of manner or hardihood of assertion is then too great for this senator.

As almost any refined southern gentleman of the time would have told you, those were fighting words! Unfortunately, Sen. Butler was ill and bed-ridden and could not respond to Sumner's attack. However, Butler's cousin, Preston Brooks, a South Carolina congressman, took it upon himself to defend his family honor.

South Carolina congressman Preston Brooks (left) and Massachusetts senator Charles Sumner (right). *Courtesy Library of Congress*

Brooks wanted to challenge Sumner to a duel. He consulted another South Carolina Congressman Lawrence Keitt about the proper dueling etiquette. Keitt responded:

> Dueling is for gentleman of equal standing. Sumner is lower than a drunkard. Dueling with him would only be an insult to yourself.

So Brooks and Keitt decided to give Sumner a "beating."

On May 22 Preston Brooks and Lawrence Keitt entered the Senate chamber. Brooks confronted Sumner, sitting at his desk. Looming over him, Brooks said:

> Mr. Sumner, I have read your speech twice over carefully. It is a libel on South Carolina, and Mr. Butler, who is a relative of mine.

As Sumner attempted to stand, Brooks swung his thick, golden-headed wood cane, at Sumner's head. After several blows the senator was bleeding profusely, almost blinded by the blood running down his face. He staggered to his feet and then collapsed unconscious on the floor.

Several senators attempted to restrain Brooks, and come to Sumner's aid, but they were blocked by Keitt, who brandished a pistol at them. Brooks continued to flail Sumner's prostrate body until the cane broke. He then quickly exited with Keitt.

Brooks was widely cheered as a hero across the South. He was sent dozens of new canes, one inscribed: "Good job," and another which read "Hit him again." Southern lawmakers made rings out of the original cane's remains, which they wore on neck chains to show their solidarity.

The *Richmond Enquirer* wrote:

> We consider the act good in conception, better in execution, and best of all in consequences. These vulgar abolitionists in the Senate must be lashed into submission.

A motion to expel Brooks from the House failed, but he resigned, stating that he:

TOP: J.L. Magee's famous political cartoon. "Southern Chivalry – Argument versus Club's". BOTTOM: Printed by John H. Bufford, Boston. Titled "Arguments of the Chivalry." The quote by Henry Ward Beecher above the image reads: "The symbol of the North is the pen; The Symbol of the South is the Bludgeon."
Courtesy Library of Congress

> Meant no disrespect to the Senate of the United States.
> Had I intended to kill Sumner I would have used a
> different weapon.

Brooks was convicted of assault by the District of Columbia and fined $300. Three months later South Carolina held a special election to fill his seat in the House and he was re-elected.

Northerners were incensed. The episode only confirmed their worst fears that no reasonable discussion about slavery could be attempted with a southerner. They claimed the South relied on "the bludgeon, the revolver, and the bowie-knife" to silence its opponents.

Sumner spent several weeks in the hospital. He spent three years at home recuperating before returning to his Senate seat, but suffered lifelong, chronic pain.

By early 1860, the issues of slavery, state's rights and secession had reached a fever pitch among the South Carolina elites and politicians. On April 24 the Democratic National Convention convened in Charleston at South Carolina Institute Hall. Caleb Cushing of Massachusetts presided over the convention. It was a volatile assembly, with most of the delegates split along sectional lines.

In his opening remarks Benjamin Perry of South Carolina said: "we have a duty to guard [the South] against evils which no one can forsee or foretell." He urged the convention to choose a candidate who would maintain the Union. His speech was greeted with hissing from the crowd.

In another speech Congressman Lawrence M. Keitt passionately defended the South's entrenched position:

> African slavery is the corner-stone of the industrial,
> social, and political fabric of the South; and whatever
> wars against it, wars against her very existence. Strike
> down the institution of African slavery and you reduce
> the South to depopulation and barbarism . . . The anti-
> slavery party contend that slavery is wrong in itself, and
> the Government is a consolidated national democracy.
> We of the South contend that slavery is right, and that
> this is a confederate Republic of sovereign States.

Slavery and states' rights were at the forefront of the Convention. Northern Democrats held firm to their belief that slavery should not expand to the western territories. Southern delegates were adamant that slave owners should be allowed to take their property (slaves) wherever they chose.

The Charleston convention ended without a Democrat presidential nominee. The delegates from eight Southern states walked out declaring "Slavery is our King – Slavery is our Truth – Slavery is our Divine Right." The remaining delegates were unable to agree on a nominee and on May 3 they voted to adjourn and reconvene in Baltimore six weeks later.

With the Democrat party splint the Northern delegates nominated Stephen Douglas as their candidate, and the Southern delegates nominated the sitting vice president, John Breckenridge from Kentucky, to challenge Republican candidate Abraham Lincoln. Adding to the confusion, there was a fourth presidential candidate, John Bell of the Constitution Union Party.

On election night, November 6, 1860, a large crowd gathered in front of City Hall in Charleston, awaiting the results to be announced. At 4:00 A.M. it was announced that Lincoln had been elected. Voter turnout was 81.2 %, the highest in American history at that point. Lincoln did not carry a single slave-holding state and received less than forty per cent of the popular vote. However with the split among the Democrats, he handily won the Electoral College.

The *Charleston Mercury* described the scene in front of City Hall:

> The crowd gave expression to their feelings by long and continued cheering for a Southern Confederacy. The greatest excitement prevailed, and the news spread with lighting rapidity over the city.

In U.S. district court on the day of Lincoln's election, Judge Andrew Magrath rose from his bench and announced:

> In the political history of the United States, an event has happened of ominous import to fifteen slaveholding states ... so far as I am concerned, the Temple of Justice, raised under the Constitution of the United States, is now closed. If it shall be never again opened, I thank God that

its doors have been closed before its altar has been desecrated with sacrifices to tyranny.

Charlestonians gather overnight at City Hall awaiting the news of the 1860 election.
Courtesy Library of Congress

Federal Port Collector W.F. Colcock was even more direct when he announced, "I will not serve under the enemy of my country."

On November 10 the South Carolina General Assembly called for a Secession Conference in Columbia. Since construction on the new State House was not complete, the Assembly met in the First Baptist Church sanctuary, the largest hall in the city.

James Petigru, a Charleston lawyer opposed to Secession, was in Columbia on business. He was stopped by a stranger who asked directions to the state insane asylum. Petigru replied, "The building, my friend, stands upon the outskirts of the town, but I think you will find the inmates yonder." He then pointed to the First Baptist Church.

1860 PRESIDENTIAL ELECTION RESULTS	
CANDIDATE / POLITICAL PARTY	PERCENTAGE OF VOTE
ABRAHAM LINCOLN (Republican Party)	**39.8 %** (1,865,908) 180 Electoral votes; 18 states carried (not a single Southern state)
JOHN BRECKINRIDGE (Southern Democrat)	**18.1%** (848,049) 72 Electoral votes; 11 states carried
STEPHEN DOUGLAS (Northern Democrat)	**29.5%** (1,380,201) 12 Electoral Votes; 1 state carried
JOHN BELL (Constitution Union / Whig)	**12.6%** (590,901) 39 Electoral votes; 3 states carried

On December 17 the Secession Convention convened. Due to an outbreak of smallpox in Columbia the 169 delegates voted to relocate to Charleston.

The next day they arrived by train and were greeted at the station with a fifteen-gun salute, the number of slave states. There was a carnival-like atmosphere at Citadel cadets escorted the delegates from the station through the cheering crowds lining the city streets.

At 1:15 in the afternoon of December 20 at St. Andrew's Hall, the Convention voted 169-0 to secede from the United States and form the Republic of South Carolina. The Charleston Mercury published a one sheet "Extra," with the screaming headline: "THE UNION IS DISSOLVED!" During the afternoon church bells pealed in celebration.

At 6:30 P.M. the Convention reconvened in South Carolina Institute Hall for the two-hour signing ceremony. Mrs. F.G. de Fontaine later described the event:

> When R.B. Rhett, the "father of secession" knelt and bowed his head in silent prayer over the document he was about to sign, there were scarcely a dry eye in the house … Two of the members … were discussing the matter later in the evening when one remarked, "Yes we had signed it in ink, but many of us will seal it in blood."

Courtesy Library of Congress

After the last signature was affixed to the document, President of the Convention, D.F. Jamison, announced:

> The Ordinance of Secession has been signed and ratified and I proclaim the State of South Carolina an Independent Commonwealth!

Charleston erupted into a night of wild celebration, including church bells pealing, pistol shots and cannon blasts from the Citadel grounds. Barrels of rosin were set fire at intersections through the city; firecrackers were lit and rockets exploded into the sky. Taverns were raucous and crowds of drunkards danced in the streets until dawn.

William Waud, of *Frank Leslie's Newspaper*, perfectly captured the Secession celebration on Meeting Street, in front of the Mills Hotel.
Courtesy Library of Congress

Murat Halstead, editor of the *Cincinnati Commercial* covered the Secession Convention. He reported:

There was a Fourth of July feeling in Charleston last night – a jubilee. There was no mistaking the public sentiment of the city. It was overwhelmingly and enthusiastically in favor of the seceders. In all her history Charleston has never enjoyed herself so hugely.

After thirty years of perceived grievances and insults, South Carolina had finally taken a long-threatened, bold and aggressive step toward a confrontation with the government of the United States of America.

Two views of South Carolina Institute Hall from Frank Leslie's Illustrated Newspaper. TOP: View of the Hall from Meeting Street. BOTTOM: View inside the Hall during the Secession signing. *Courtesy Library of Congress*

34 1861 FIRST SHOT(S) OF THE WAR BETWEEN THE STATES

For 150 years there has been a minor skirmish among historians as to *"when"* the first shot of the War Beween the States was fired. There is consensus that the first shot was fired in Charleston; the problem is that there are two dates vying for the prize.

- ✝ JANUARY 9, 1861: an unarmed civilian supply ship *Star of the West* was fired on attempting to resupply the Federal troops at Ft. Sumter.
- ✝ APRIL 12, 1861: Confederate forces fired on the United States garrison at Fort Sumter.

Both stories are presented here; in fact, both are merely episodes in a larger story, and you, the reader, can form your own opinion about which date deserves the honor.

FIRST SHOT #1

The Union merchant ship, *Star of the West,* was built by Jeremiah Simonson of New York for Cornelius Vanderbilt. It was a 1,172 ton, two-deck ship, a length of 228.3 feet, a beam of 32.7 feet, with double wooden hullside paddle wheels and two masts.

When South Carolina seceded December 20, 1860, (see #33), newly elected Governor Francis Pickens demanded the immediate withdrawal of the Federal garrison at Fort Moultrie. President James Buchanan, a Democrat, refused but was also careful not to make a provocative move that could be misinterpreted.

Several weeks before Secession, due to the enflamed rhetoric coming from South Carolina leaders, the Buchanan administration found it prudent to investigate the readiness of military installations throughout the South. Major Fitz John Porter was dispatched to inspect the Charleston fortifications. What he discovered was disturbing.

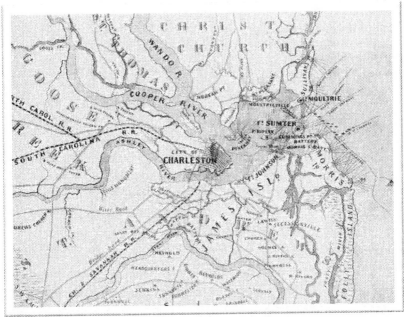

Map of Charleston fortifications, 1861. *Courtesy Library of Congress*

One quarter of the garrison at Fort Moultrie was either under arrest or confined for disciplinary reasons. There was also no sentinel on watch, making the fort vulnerable to attack from shore. Castle Pinckney, in Charleston harbor, was manned by a single ordinance officer Lt. R.K. Meade. Fort Sumter, under construction for more than three decades, was still unfinished.

In an effort to upgrade the Federal readiness, Major Robert Anderson was ordered to replace the elderly Col. John L. Gardner as commander of the Charleston garrison.

Anderson, from Kentucky, graduated from the U.S. Military Academy in 1825. During the Black Hawk War of 1832 he served as colonel in command of the Illinois volunteers, among them a young Abraham Lincoln. He was regarded as a professional, level-headed and discreet officer. His family had once owned slaves and he was married to a woman from Georgia. President Buchanan hoped that placing a proslavery Southerner in charge would be seen as a conciliatory move by the South Carolina firebrands.

Anderson arrived on November 19 and discovered that South Carolina was already preparing for war. Workmen were constructing a floating ironclad battery for the harbor and a land battery on Morris Island. The Federal government had also informed outgoing South Carolina governor, William Gist, it was going to send more men and arms to Charleston. Gist replied on November 29:

> I have found great difficulty in restraining the people of Charleston from seizing the forts, and have only been able to restrain them by the assurance that no additional troops would be sent to the forts, or any munitions of war ... [if the President sends reinforcements] the responsibility will rest on him of lighting the torch of discord, which will only be quenched in blood.

Anderson himself wrote, "The storm may break upon us at any moment." The next day, Anderson ordered his second in command, Capt. John Foster Gray, U.S. Engineers, to resume work on Fort Sumter. The barracks was unfinished, and only 15 of the 135 guns were mounted. In Anderson's opinion, "It should be garrisoned at once." More than 115 men were put to work under the direction of Gray.

Anderson dispatched a detachment to Charleston to secure a six months' supply of rations. The soldiers were harassed by locals as soon as they tied up at the wharf. One of the Federal officers wrote, "The secessionists could hardly be restrained from attacking us." To say the least, tensions between the Federal troops and the citizens of Charleston was rapidly becoming volatile.

On December 7, 1860, Anderson received an order from the Secretary of War:

> You are carefully to avoid every act which would needlessly tend to provoke aggression; and for that reason you are not, without evident and imminent necessity, to take up any position which could be

construed into the assumption of a hostile attitude. But you are to hold possession of the forts of this harbor, and if attacked you are to defend yourself to the last extremity.

The smallness of your force will not permit you, perhaps, to occupy more than one of the three forts, but an attack on or an attempt to take possession of any one of them will be regarded as an act of hostility ...

Major Robert Anderson. *Courtesy Library of Congress*

Two weeks later, December 20, South Carolina seceded. The Federal garrison at Fort Moultrie could clearly hear the celebration taking place three miles away across the harbor, skyrockets and bonfires were visible. Anderson realized he was now stationed within enemy territory. He made the decision to abandon Moultrie and consolidate his force at Sumter.

That same day, in Washington, D.C., a letter was delivered to President Buchanan from Governor Francis Pickens. Marked "STRICTLY CONFIDENTIAL," Pickens asked permission for South Carolina "to take over Fort Sumter in Charleston Harbor ... with a sincere desire to prevent a collision of force." Without addressing the issue of Sumter, Buchanan's reply simply requested for more time to deliberate.

At sundown, December 26, 1860, Anderson ordered his men to pack everything and prepare to move within half an hour. Three miles away in Charleston, Christmas celebrations were still taking place in many of the homes. Over the next hour, taking advantage of the holiday laxness and the cover of darkness, the entire garrison relocated from Ft. Moultrie across the narrow channel to Fort Sumter.

As they were leaving, a small detachment spiked the cannons, burned the gun carriages that faced Fort Sumter and cut down the flagstaff.

The next morning Charleston awoke to an American flag flying over Fort Sumter and smoldering fires at Fort Moultrie. An embarrassed, and enraged Governor Pickens demanded that Anderson return to Moultrie. Anderson politely declined.

Gov. Pickens ordered that Castle Pinckney by seized to "protect public property." Local troops led by Colonel James Pettigrew landed at Castle Pinckney that afternoon. Lt. Meade, the only person stationed there, put up no resistance.

Castle Pinckney was commandeered and Meade was released. As the Palmetto flag was raised over Pinckney he was allowed to go to Fort Sumter. Utilizing their field glasses, Major Anderson and Captain Abner Doubleday had watched the seizure from the ramparts of Fort Sumter. Anderson viewed this as an act of war, but

Anderson and Federal troops enter Ft. Sumter. *Courtesy Library of Congress*

Federal troops spike the guns at Ft. Moultrie. *Courtesy Library of Congress*

heeding his orders to be cautious, he did nothing.

Two days later General Winfield Scott, Commander of the U.S. Army, told President Buchanan that Anderson needed reinforcements to hold Sumter. Buchanan did nothing.

Castle Pinckney in Charleston harbor taken by South Carolina troops.
Courtesy Library of Congress

On December 30, South Carolina troops seized the Charleston Arsenal and three days later, Fort Johnson on James Island. At the insistence of Governor Pickens, a battery was hastily built at Johnson. It was manned by two hundred militia and fifty Citadel cadets trained in artillery. Within a week the cadets managed to build a battery of twenty-four pounders, facing east, hidden behind dunes and sand bags.

Anderson, with no word from Washington, ordered the main gate installed at Fort Sumter, and the cannons mounted. During the next several days the seventy men inside Sumter placed several cannons, finished the brickwork and put the fort on a defensive footing.

All of these activities took place in plain view of the Charleston citizenry.

Early in January, President Buchanan finally made a decision. Since Anderson needed supplies, and the president was still attempting to keep events from spinning out of control, he decided to send an unarmed ship, *Star of the West*, loaded with supplies and 250 volunteers.

The *Star* left New York on January 5, 1861. After the ship was en route, Anderson sent word to Secretary of War Joseph Holt that supplies were not needed. Holt tried in vain to recall the *Star*.

Anderson may have been the only person unaware that the ship was on its way. It was certainly no secret in Charleston. On January 6 the *Charleston Mercury* wrote:

> Despatches [sic] from New York say that the steamer *Star of the West* of the Panama line, coaled up yesterday with unusual celerity. The rumor is that she is to carry troops to Charleston, but this is ridiculed at the Steamship Company's Office.

Two days later the *Mercury* reported, in all capital letters:

> UNITED STATES TROOPS HASTENING FROM ALL POINTS SOUTHWARD. THE *STAR OF THE WEST*, WITH REINFORCEMENT FOR ANDERSON, DUE HERE TODAY.

Charleston was feverish with excitement. Many locals spent their afternoons sitting on their piazzas, or the roof of their mansions, looking out to sea with spyglasses.

A few minutes past six in the morning, January 9, Captain John McGowan of the *Star*, steered the ship into the channel near Fort Sumter, passing Morris Island. All soldiers were out of sight below decks, with only the civilian crew visible. The hope was to sneak past the Rebel forces on Morris Island.

It was just after reveille when Confederate sentries spotted the *Star*. Major Peter F. Stevens gave the order, "Commence firing." Two cannon shots, fired by cadet gunner George E. Haynesworth, roared from a South Carolina battery, skipped in front of the *Star* and sunk harmlessly in the water.

Star of the West, an unarmed civilian supply ship. *Courtesy Library of Congress.*

Firing on the *Star of the West* from Fort Johnson, January 9, 1861.
Courtesy Library of Congress

Over the next ten minutes, the *Star* continued to take fire. Captain McGowan reported:

> One shot just passed clear of the pilot-house, another passed between the smoke-stack ad walking-beams of the engine, another struck the ship just abaft the fore-rigging and stove in the planking, while another came within an ace of carrying away the rudder.

Anderson ordered his garrison to battle stations. Having received no instructions from Washington, he ordered his officers to hold fire. With no covering fire from Sumter, McGowan ordered the *Star* to reverse course and exit the harbor. In all, seventeen shots were fired and the entire episode lasted forty-five minutes.

The next morning, the *Charleston Mercury* crowed:

> Yesterday will be remembered in history. The expulsion of the *Star of the West* from Charleston Harbor yesterday morning was the opening ball of the Revolution. We are proud that our harbor has been so honored. The State of South Carolina, so long and so bitterly reviled and scoffed at has thrown back her enemies.

Anderson informed his superiors in Washington that he needed 20,000 troops to hold Charleston Harbor. The War Department responded:

> You will continue, as heretofore, to act strictly on the defensive, and to avoid, by all means compatible with the safety of your command, a collision with the hostile forces by which you surrounded.

Lt. Smith, on board the *Star of the West* humorously wrote:

> The people of Charleston pride themselves on their hospitality, but it exceeded our expectations. They gave us several balls before we landed.

FIRST SHOT #2

On January 23, 1861 Pierre Gustave Toutant Beauregard was appointed superintendent of the U.S. Military Academy at West Point. Five days after taking the position, his home state, Louisiana, seceded. The Federal powers-that-be did not trust Beauregard's southern sympathies, so the next day his commission as superintendent was revoked, making his tenure the shortest ever at West Point. One month later, Beauregard resigned his captaincy in the U.S. Army Engineers and offered his services to the Confederate government being formed in Montgomery, Alabama.

Beauregard was born into a prominent Creole family in St. Bernard Parish, Louisiana and raised on a sugarcane plantation outside of New Orleans. At the age of sixteen, in 1834, he was appointed to the United States Military Academy. He quickly became a popular cadet, earning several nicknames including "Little Napoleon" and "Little Creole," due to his slight statue – 5'7" and 150-pounds. His favorite teacher was his professor of artillery, Robert Anderson. When Beauregard graduated second in his class in 1838 he remained at the school to serve as Anderson's assistant artillery instructor.

During the Mexican-American War he served under Gen. Winfield Scott and during the 1850s worked as a military engineer clearing the Mississippi River of obstruction.

On February 27, 1861, in Montgomery, Alabama, Beauregard was appointed the first brigadier general of the Confederate Army. By this time, six other Southern states - Mississippi, Florida, Alabama, Georgia, Louisiana and Texas – had joined South Carolina and were in the process of establishing a government and an army. Beauregard was ordered to assume command of "all forces in and about Charleston Harbor."

He arrived March 3, met with Governor Pickens and inspected the harbor defenses finding them "to be in disarray." He understood that his primary goal was to persuade his former instructor to evacuate Fort Sumter.

Beauregard moved into the second floor of the Mills House Hotel and sent several cases of fine brandy and whiskey as well as boxes of cigars to Anderson and his officers. Anderson ordered the gifts returned.

Pierre Gustave Toutant Beauregard. *Courtesy Library of Congress*

On March 4, in his inaugural address, President Abraham Lincoln stated he was "resolved to hold, occupy and possess the property and places belonging to the government."

In a letter written on the same day, Major Anderson notified the War Department in Washington that he could hold the fort until April 15, at which time most supplies would be exhausted. He reported that he was "surrounded by battle emplacements and needed substantial reinforcements to hold Sumter." He also noted that he was no longer able to buy food in Charleston and would "need to be resupplied within six weeks or the men would have to go on short rations."

Charleston, South Carolina, 1861, soldiers marching down Broad Street toward the Exchange Building. Fort Sumter is visible in the distance.
Courtesy Library of Congress

Confederate authorities in Charleston decided that on or by April 15, Fort Sumter must be either evacuated, or seized. Confederate President Jefferson Davis issued an order to Beauregard:

> You will demand its evacuation and, if this is refused, proceed in such manner as you may determine to reduce it.

Charleston itself was caught up in an atmosphere that was part anticipation and part apprehension. Despite the daily parties, military balls, grand luncheons and teas, this sense of frivolity was balanced with a dreadful uncertainty as everyone waited for politicians to stop waltzing around the issues that could easily lead to hostilities.

In April Emma Holmes, daughter of a wealthy planter living in Charleston, wrote in her diary:

> We walked to visit the fortifications ... the gentlemen had provided us with fruit cake and champagne for lunch ... dinner was laid in a tent and was very nice, but camp life was shown by the deficiency of china ... boned turkey, ham, lobster, salad, etc, but laid out in camp fashion – all the dessert being on at the same time ... fresh preserved peaches, jelly and pound cake and afterwards ice cream and of course champagne and wines.

Mary Chesnut, wife of Col. James Chesnut, second in command to Beauregard, wrote on April 6:

> The plot thickens, the air is red hot with rumors ... In spite of all, Tom Huger came for us and we went on the *Planter* to take a look at Morris Island ...

A reporter for the *New York Times* wrote about the attitude among the city's elite. He suggested that a doctor be sent to the city to "give us a proper analysis of them." He also reported:

> The more I see of the men of Charleston, the more convinced I am that very many of them act, talk and behave like perfect children ... Charleston is a sublime mystery not measured by any of the common-sense rules that govern one in their intercourse with ordinary people.

On April 6, President Lincoln notified Governor Pickens and Beauregard that he had sent a naval expedition to resupply Fort Sumter, including 200 reinforcements. President Jefferson Davis ordered Beauregard to prevent those provisions from being delivered.

On April 11, Beauregard sent a letter to Major Anderson demanding the surrender of the fort. The letter was carried by Col. James Chesnut, Alexander Chisolm and Stephen Dill Lee. Their boat, carrying a white flag, docked at Ft. Sumter at 3:34 P.M. and they were escorted to the guardroom, just inside the gate. The note from Beauregard read:

SIR: The Government of the Confederate States has hitherto forborne from any hostile demonstration against Fort Sumter, in the hope that the Government of the United States, with a view to the amicable adjustment of all questions between the two Governments, and to avert the calamities of war, would voluntarily evacuate it.

There was reason at one time to believe that such would be the course pursued by the Government of the United States, and under that impression my Government has refrained from making any demand for the surrender of the fort. But the Confederate States can no longer delay assuming actual possession of a fortification commanding the entrance of one of their harbors, and necessary to its defense and security.

I am ordered by the Government of the Confederate States to demand the evacuation of Fort Sumter. My aides, Colonel Chesnut and Captain Lee, are authorized to make such demand of you. All proper facilities will be afforded for the removal of yourself and command, together with company arms and property, and all private property, to any post in the United States which you may select. The flag which you have upheld so long and with so much fortitude, under the most trying circumstances, may be saluted by you on taking it down.

Colonel Chesnut and Captain Lee will for a reasonable time, await your answer.

I am, sir, very respectfully, your obedient servant,

G. T. BEAUREGARD,
Brigadier-General, Commanding.

Federal officers at Fort Sumter. BACK ROW, L-R: Capt. Seymour, 1st Lt. Snyder, 1st Lt. Davis, 2nd Lt. Meade, 1st Lt. Talbot. FRONT ROW, L-R: Capt. Doubleday, Major Anderson, Asst. Surgeon Crawford, Capt. Foster. *Courtesy Library of Congress*

Anderson read the note to his officers and they agreed to reject the Confederate's ultimatum. About 4:30 P.M. Anderson handed his response to Chesnut and the Confederate aides boarded their boat to carry it back to Beauregard.

As they were leaving, Anderson asked, "Will General Beauregard open his batteries without further notice to me?"

Col. Chesnut, a former U.S. Senator and therefore the most senior of the aides answered, "No, I can say to you that he will not, without giving further notice."

Anderson replied, "Gentlemen, if you do not batter the fort to pieces about us, we shall be starved out in a few days." Anderson was sending Beauregard a subtle message: if the resupply effort from Washington was unsuccessful, he would be the one to make the decision whether or not to surrender the fort.

James Chesnut and Stephen Dill Lee, Confederate aides-de-camp to Gen. Beauregard.
Courtesy Library of Congress

While these events at Fort Sumter were playing out, in downtown Charleston, rumors spread that something was about to happen. Emma Holmes described it in her diary:

> A day never to be forgotten in the annals of Charleston ... the whole afternoon & night the Battery was thronged with spectators of every age and sex, anxiously watching and awaiting with the momentary expectation of hearing the war of cannon opening on the fort or on the fleet

which was reported off the bar. Everybody was restless and all who could go were out.

At about 5:30 P.M., Chesnut delivered Anderson's note to Beauregard. It read:

> GENERAL: I have the honor to acknowledge the receipt of your communication demanding the evacuation of this fort, and to say, in reply thereto, that it is a demand with which I regret that my sense of honor, and of my obligations to my Government, prevent my compliance. Thanking you for the fair, manly, and courteous terms proposed, and for the high compliment paid me.
>
> I am, general, very respectfully, your obedient servant,
>
> ROBERT ANDERSON,
> Major, First Artillery, Commanding.

After contacting his superiors in Montgomery, Beauregard wrote another dispatch, and about midnight, his aides rowed out to Fort Sumter again flying a white flag. His response to Anderson was:

> MAJOR: In consequence of the verbal observation made by you to my aides, Messrs. Chesnut and Lee, in relation to the condition of your supplies, and that you would in a few days be starved out if our guns did not batter you to pieces, or words to that effect, and desiring no useless effusion of blood, I communicated both the verbal observations and your written answer to my communications to my Government.
>
> If you will state the time at which you will evacuate Fort Sumter, and agree that in the mean time you will not use your guns against us unless ours shall be employed against Fort Sumter, we will abstain from opening fire upon you. Colonel Chesnut and Captain Lee are authorized by me to enter into such an agreement with

you. You are, therefore, requested to communicate to them an open answer.

I remain, major, very respectfully, your obedient servant,

G. T. BEAUREGARD,
Brigadier-General, Commanding.

About 1:30 A.M. Anderson assembled his officers and read the Confederacy's latest offer. For the next ninety minutes they discussed a response. They all considered the condition that they would not fire unless fired upon to be unacceptable. If the Federal supply ship arrived, Confederate batteries would no doubt open fire. The Federal officers were determined not to repeat their lack of response during the *Star of the West* episode. But they were unsure of when - or even if - the supply ship would arrive. The officers agreed they could hold out four more days. Anderson composed his next reply to Beauregard:

GENERAL: I have the honor to acknowledge the receipt by Colonel Chesnut of your second communication of the 11th instant, and to state in reply that, cordially uniting with you in the desire to avoid the useless effusion of blood, I will, if provided with the proper and necessary means of transportation, evacuate Fort Sumter by noon on the 15th instant, and that I will not in the meantime open my fires upon your forces unless compelled to do so by some hostile act against this fort or the flag of my Government by the forces under your command, or by some portion of them, or by the perpetration of some act showing a hostile intention on your part against this fort or the flag it bears, should I not receive prior to that time controlling instructions from my Government or additional supplies.

I am, general, very respectfully, your obedient servant,

ROBERT ANDERSON,
Major, First Artillery, Commanding.

The Confederate aides Chesnut, Chisholm and Lee read the reply immediately. Chesnut, following Beauregard's orders, composed the following note:

> SIR: By authority of Brigadier-General Beauregard, commanding the Provisional Forces of the Confederate States, we have the honor to notify you that he will open the fire of his batteries on Fort Sumter in one hour from this time.
>
> We have the honor to be, very respectfully, your obedient servants.
>
> JAMES CHESNUT, JR.,
> Aide-de-Camp.
> STEPHEN D. LEE,
> Captain, C. S. Army, Aide-de-Camp.

Chesnut delivered the message to Anderson. After reading it, Anderson pulled out his pocket watch and checked the time: it was 3:20 A.M. He asked Chesnut, "I understand you, sir, then, that your batteries will open in an hour from this time?"

Chesnut replied, "Yes, sir. In one hour."

Anderson walked the Confederate officers to their boat. It was beginning to rain. He shook hands with each of them. "Gentlemen, if we do not meet again in this world, I hope we may meet in a better one," he told them.

Inside Fort Sumter Anderson ordered his men to prepare for an attack within the hour. He urged them to sleep if possible, as they would be returning fire at dawn.

The Confederate officers made the one-mile journey from Sumter to Johnson within half an hour. Col. Chesnut told Captain George James, battery commander at Johnson, they had given Anderson a deadline, and it was to be met. He was to fire a signal shot at 4:30 A.M.

Chestnut, Lee and Chisholm, anxious to return to Beauregard as soon as possible, then got back in their boat and began to row across the harbor. Out in the middle of the water, in the drizzling rain, not a single star was visible against the dark forbidding sky. At exactly 4:30 A.M., Lt. Henry S. Farley pulled the lanyard on one of the cannons at the beach battery on James Island. A mortar shell arced high across the water, heading for Ft. Sumter, its burning fuse leaving a glowing contrail, illuminating the sky. It exploded just above the fort like Fourth of July fireworks, spreading an orange-red glow across the horizon.

Confederate batteries at Fort Johnson fire on Fort Sumter, April 12, 1861.
Courtesy Library of Congress

Within a minute of the signal shot, another shell screamed across the harbor and exploded within Fort Sumter. Beauregard had given precise orders on the firing rhythm. The forty-three guns that faced Sumter were each to fire in turn, in a counterclockwise pattern, with two minutes between each shot, in order to save shot and powder.

In Charleston, Chesnut's wife, Mary, was having a restless night. As she wrote in her diary:

I do not pretend to sleep. How can I? If Anderson does not accept terms at four, the orders are he shall be fired upon. I count four, St. Michael's bells chime out and I begin to hope. At half-past four the heavy booming of a cannon. I sprang out of bed, and on my knees prostrate prayed as I have never prayed before ... I knew my husband was rowing about in a boat somewhere in that dark bay, and that the shells were roofing it over, bursting toward the fort. The women were wild out there on the housetop.

Watching the bombardment from Charleston rooftops.
Courtesy Library of Congress

In Charleston, the bombardment was a spectacle. As dawn broke, the streets were filled with people rushing in the rain to find a vantage point from which to watch the battle. The sea wall along the Battery was quickly crammed with ladies and gentlemen in their finest clothes. Boys scampered around, climbing on anything in an attempt to have a better view of the harbor.

There was not a single person who believed the Yankees would win.

Confederate soldiers keeping watch on the Battery during the bombardment.
Courtesy Library of Congress

School teacher Anna Brackett described the scene in Charleston:

> Women of all ages and ranks of life look eagerly out with spyglasses and opera glasses. Children talk and laugh and walk back and forth in the small moving place as if they were at a public show.

As dawn broke just after six, the Federal garrison at Sumter mustered for roll call and breakfast, which consisted mainly of salt pork. Private Joe Thompson wrote: "Our supply of foodstuffs are fast giving out. Yesterday our allowance was one biscuit."

At 6:30 A.M. Capt. Doubleday ordered the first Federal shot to be aimed at the Iron Battery on Cummings Point. It landed beyond the battery and in the marsh.

By full light the rain had stopped and for the next two days, Fort Sumter was hammered from three sides by Confederate batteries, with more than 2,500 shots fired the first day. Overnight the bombardment slackened but resumed in full force the next morning.

By 8:00 A.M. on April 13, the upper story of Sumter's officer's quarters were burning. The most immediate danger was the 300 barrels of gunpowder stored in a magazine. At one o'clock the flagstaff at Fort Sumter was struck by a Confederate shell and crashed to the ground. The soldiers rushed to rehoist the flag before the Rebels assumed they had surrendered.

At about this time, another Beauregard aide, former Senator Col. Louis Wigfall of Texas was at Cummings Point, watching the bombardment with growing restlessness. He developed a deep admiration for Anderson and the Federal garrison. As he described his feelings: "Anderson is a damned rascal … but he is brave & he has shown pluck."

Watching the flames inside Sumter grow larger, the Confederates decided that a boat should go over to Sumter. Wigfall immediately volunteered and had himself rowed out by three slaves. Soldiers at Sumter were perplexed a man waving a white handkerchief from a sword approaching their fort. The Federals raised a flag of truce and Wigfall, although he had no authority to do so, told the first Federal officers he met, "Let us stop this firing. You are on fire, and your flag is down. Let us quit."

Anderson arrived a moment later and Wigfall told him:

> You have defended your flag nobly sir. You have done all that it is possible to do, and General Beauregard wants to stop this fight. On what terms, Major Anderson, will you evacuate this fort?

Anderson replied: "General Beauregard is already acquainted with my terms." He felt some relief. His soldiers were half-starved, exhausted and down to their last three shots. The American flag was taken down and Wigfall's white handkerchief was raised in its place. The firing from all batteries ceased – the battle over.

Inside Fort Sumter during the bombardment. *Courtesy Library of Congress*

Church bells rang throughout the city. Men on horseback galloped across the city, shouting the glorious news. Spectators on the Battery sea wall cheered hysterically, the sound carrying across the harbor to the exhausted soldiers in Fort Sumter.

The next day at noon, April 14, the Federal garrison at Sumter saluted the American flag with a fifty-gun salute. The harbor was filled with thousands of Charlestonians, on every type of boat imaginable, to watch the surrender.

The *New York Times* correspondent described the scene:

> The bells have been chiming all day, guns firing, ladies waving handkerchiefs, people cheering and citizens making themselves generally demonstrative. It is regarded as the greatest day in the history of South Carolina.

Interior of Fort Sumter, Confederate flag flying after the surrender.
Courtesy Library of Congress

35 1864   FIRST SUCCESSFUL SUBMARINE ATTACK

At 8:45 P.M. on February 17, 1864, the Confederate submarine *H.L. Hunley* attacked and sank the *U.S.S Housatonic*, just outside Charleston harbor. It was the first successful submarine attack in world history. Unfortunately, the *Hunley* never returned from its mission. Its crew of eight were all lost.

The story of the *Hunley* spans more than 150 years. Beginning with its construction, proceeding through tragic test runs, climaxing with a successful mission and mysterious disappearance, reemerging from a watery grave and ending with its painstaking restoration, the chronicle of the Confederate submarine is the stuff of legends.

Horace L. Hunley was a wealthy, prominent lawyer and planter, who served in the Louisiana state legislature. Southern patriotism inspired him to support the Confederate War effort, and he poured much of his personal wealth into the cause. In June 1861 he led a blockade-running mission to Cuba for munitions and arms.

Then he met James McClintock, an ingenious young engineer. As a youth McClintock joined the crew of a Mississippi river boat and by the time of the Civil War, he was known as "the youngest steamboat captain on the river." He also developed skills as an engineer and inventor. When he found himself stuck in New Orleans due to the War, he started a business, constructing steam gauges in a machine shop just off the French Quarter.

By the fall of 1861 Hunley and McClintock attempted the construction of a "fish-boat," a submersible that might help combat the superior power of the Union Navy. With Hunley and other southern patriots bankrolling the effort, McClintock used an old iron boiler – 34 feet long, 4 feet wide and 4 feet tall – to construct the hull.

The vessel, named the *Pioneer,* could accommodate a crew of three, two facing one another while cranking the screw propeller and the third standing in the conning tower, steering with ropes attached to the rudder and simple diving fins.

They tested the *Pioneer* on Lake Pontchartrain. It was slow, making only two knots, nowhere close to the speed needed to attack much faster Union vessels. There was also no way to transport the four-ton boat overland. Despite its severe limitations, the Confederate government was intrigued by the possibilities and issued a privateering license to Hunley and McClintock.

When New Orleans was surrendered to the Union in May 1862, the fate of the *Pioneer* was sealed. They sank the boat in a deep channel and fled to Mobile, Alabama, where soon after they walked into the machine shop of Thomas Park and Thomas Lyons, who were weapon makers for the Confederacy. As Hunley and McClintock explained their plans to construct a second, improved "fish-boat", George Dixon, a young man working in the shop immediately became interested and excited.

Dixon was a recently promoted second lieutenant in the Confederate Army. However, his war-related injuries had required him to employ his mechanical talents at the shop. In a story of unbelievable luck, which would later take on mythic proportions, on April 6, 1862, during the battle of Shiloh, a bullet impacted Dixon's thigh with such force he felt as if his leg was on fire and he passed out from the pain. Luckily, the bullet had struck a $20 gold coin in his pants pocket, placing a permanent dent in the piece. The coin had been a gift from his girlfriend, Queenie Bennett, on the day he left with the Twenty-first Alabama on their way to Tennessee. Instead of having a leg blown off, he suffered a wound that left him with a limp the rest of his life. The coin had saved his life.

When he awoke and realized his amazing stroke of luck, Dixon decided was never going to be without the coin, his personal good luck charm. He carried it in his pocket and grew into the habit of rubbing it with his fingers. He actually had the coin inscribed: "Shiloh, April 6, 1862. My life preserver. G.E.D."

During the summer of 1862, the machine shop employees built the new boat, named *American Diver.* With the ever cautious McClintock in charge, the *Diver* performed well during trial runs in

Mobile Bay, with Dixon as part of the test crew. However, their attempt to attack and sink a Union ship failed. As the *Diver* was being towed to its destination near Sand Island, a violent storm suddenly appeared and Hunley, McClintock and the crew watched the *Diver* sink in the Mobile Bay waters.

Determined that their concept was sound, McClintock and Hunley immediately began designing a third boat. Using their past achievements - and failures - the new boat was engineered with a much improved design.

The main hull was a railroad boiler – four feet wide and twenty-five feet long – cut in half lengthwise, with two 12-inch iron strips were added on either side. They also added two tapered iron plates fore and aft, enabling the boat to move more easily through the water. A hand crank was installed for propulsion, with a tiller similar to the previous models. To increase its speed, the boat was designed for seven men to operate the cranks.

Tanks at each end of the vessel could be opened manually and flooded to allow the boat to submerge. Hand-operated pumps could be used to expel water to allow it to surface. The finished boat was sixty inches wide, about thirty-feet long, and five-feet tall. They christened it the *H.L. Hunley*.

The South had already constructed a small fleet of semi-submersible torpedo boats called "Davids" which lay very low in the water and their attacks on Union ships achieved varying degrees of success.

The original *David* was built from a design by St. Julien Ravenel of Charleston. The operation of a semi-submersible was simple: water was taken into ballast tanks to make it ride low in the water minimizing visibility. At night it would appear to be nothing more than a piece of floating debris. Eventually more than twenty torpedo boats were constructed. The boats carried an explosive charge composed of 134 pounds of gunpowder at the end of a spar that projected forward from the bow.

By this time, Gen. Beauregard was back in command of Charleston forces and attempting to clear the city of the Union naval blockade using the *Davids*. He was desperate. Charleston had been strangled by the blockade for almost two years, utilizing more than a dozen Federal ships. The city - indeed the entire South - was feeling the economic pinch. There was virtually no foreign trade and the Confederacy realized that no matter how many battles Rebel soldiers won, the South was losing badly on the economic front.

CSS David - one of the semi-submersible torpedo boats utilized by the Confederacy. Pictured here, one abandoned in Charleston.
Courtesy Library of Congress

Charleston, in particular, was a popular target, not only for Union forces, but for the civilian population in the North. As the main proponent for secession and the site of the first shot, hatred toward Charleston was fierce. They wanted Charleston to suffer severely.

The *Hunley* was ordered to Charleston to assist in the port defense. It was cut in half, loaded on railcars and camouflaged for the overland journey, with scaffolding build over the vessel for concealment. Dixon, however, was left behind in Mobile. A new crew would be assembled in Charleston to operate the boat, with McClintock in charge of training.

FIRST CREW

The *Hunley* arrived in Charleston August 12, 1863. McClintock was offered $100,000 ($1.6. million in current dollars) to sink either the *New Ironsides* or the *Wabash*, two of the Federal blockade ships. With a crew of volunteers, McClintock conducted a week of uneventful tests in the harbor between forts Johnson and Moultrie, away from the eyes of the blockade fleet. Beauregard quickly became frustrated by McClintock's caution. He asked that a Confederate sailor serve on the submarine. When McClintock refused, Beauregard ordered the submarine seized by the Confederate Navy and a crew of volunteers took over its operation.

McClintock was so disgusted he left the city.

On August 29, a crew of eight Confederate Navy volunteers, commanded by Lt. John A. Payne, boarded the *Hunley*. As they were releasing the lines, the Confederate ship, *Etiwan*, came steaming by. The wake from the ship washed over the *Hunley* and water poured through its open hatches. Four crew members, including Payne, escaped but the other five drowned inside the submerged vessel.

Three days later Beauregard gave orders to "adopt immediate measures to have it raised at once."

SECOND CREW

Horace Hunley arrived in Charleston that day and was stunned to discover that for the third time in two years, one of his submarines had sunk. When he discovered the particulars of the accident, he was enraged. He blamed the incident on government ineptitude. He wrote a curt note to Beauregard:

> Sir – I am part owner of the torpedo boat the *Hunley*. I have been interested in building this description of boat since the beginning of the war ... I feel therefore, a deep interest in its success. I propose if you will place the boat in my hands to furnish a crew (in whole or in part) from Mobile who are well acquainted with its management and make the attempt to destroy a vessel of the enemy as early as practicable.
>
> Very respectfully, Your Obedient Servant,
> H.L. Hunley

Within a week, Hunley took charge of his boat, after its salvage from 42-feet of water. The first order of business was the removal of the bodies of the five drowned crew members. Their bodies were so bloated limbs had to be severed for removal. It was horrific and grisly work. More days were spent with soap and brushes, cleaning the inside of the boat and removing the silt, mud and stench of decaying flesh. Many of the soldiers began to call *Hunley* the "iron coffin."

Hunley telegraphed the Mobile machine shop, asking that workers familiar with the boat be sent to Charleston. Within a few days, six men arrived. Much to George Dixon's dismay, the wounded officer was not one them. For more than a month, Hunley drilled the crew in the operation of the submarine, until the operation of the vessel was smooth and orderly.

On October 15, 1863, Horace Hunley and seven crew members boarded the submarine at Adger's Wharf. There was a small crowd assembled on the dock to watch a demonstration of the *Hunley's* capabilities, a dress rehearsal for an actual attack. The crew were to take the submarine out into the harbor, submerge beneath the Confederate ship *Indian Chief* and surface on the other side.

The crowd watched the *Hunley* cruise away from the dock, submerge but ... it never resurfaced. The next day, the *Charleston Daily Courier* posted this notice:

> MELANCHOLY OCCURRENCE – On Thursday morning an accident occurred to a small boat in Cooper River, containing eight persons, all of whom drowned.

When word reached the Mobile machine shop, all the men were shocked. The lives of George Dixon and William Alexander, two of the original test crew, had been saved by the luck of not being chosen to go to Charleston. However, they knew the boat would be raised to recover the bodies, and were confident that the *Hunley* could be used successfully. They left for Charleston the next day.

Beauregard ordered that the submarine be raised and then grounded. It had killed thirteen Confederates, and not a single Yankee. "It is more dangerous to those who use it than the enemy," he said.

Due to weather conditions in Charleston harbor, it took more than a month for the recovery. It was 60-feet below the surface, its nose buried in silt. On Saturday, November 7, several divers, including Angus Smith who had worked on the first recovery, managed to wrap enough chains around the vessel to raise it. When the *Hunley* was finally on the dock at Mt. Pleasant, Dixon and

Alexander were present for the grim task of removing the eight corpses.

Beauregard wrote, "It was indescribably ghastly. The unfortunate men were contorted into all kinds of horrible attitudes."

THIRD CREW & HISTORIC MISSION

Despite Beauregard's misgivings, Dixon and Alexander, however, were not ready to give up on the submarine. They managed to set up a meeting with the general at his residence, 192 Ashley Avenue. Dixon had served under Beauregard at Shiloh, and the general knew Dixon to be a serious and resolute soldier. They convinced him that failure to use the vessel would be a missed opportunity. Dixon pointed out that the *Hunley* had sank most recently because the crew forgot to shut off the ballast-tank valves. The latest accident was just that and there was nothing wrong with the submarine itself, as long as it was properly operated.

Dixon told Beauregard that with him in command, Alexander as his first officer and a crew of their choosing, the *Hunley* could and *would* sink a Union ship. Beauregard gave Dixon and Alexander permission to prepare the boat and raise a crew, but only volunteers.

It took more than a month to ready the submarine. As before, the bloated bodies had to be removed in pieces, and the interior of the vessel was cleaned with twenty-one pounds of soap and lime. All the hatches were left open for several days in an attempt air out the stench.

Dixon and Alexander were able to enlist most of the new crew from the *Indian Chief,* the same ship the *Hunley* was attempting to submerge beneath when it sank. They explained how dangerous the mission was going to be and that it would involve twelve-hour days of hard labor in a claustrophobic environment, often pitch black, in cold, wet, cramped quarters with stale air. He only wanted men willing to work under those conditions.

Dixon and Alexander supervised the Hunley's refitting. One of the main alterations, at Beauregard's order, was the replacement of the tugged mine with a mounted spar housing an explosive at the end. They also moved the submarine to Battery Marshall, at the northern end of Sullivan's Island, across from Breach Inlet on Long

Island (present-day Isle of Palms.) This took the boat away from prying eyes in Charleston harbor during their nighttime training sessions. More importantly, it was also closer to the open ocean, making for easier access to the Federal blockading fleet.

A 1902 sepia-wash drawing of Conrad Wise Chapman's painting of the *Hunley*, by R.G. Skerrett. *Courtesy Naval Historical Center.*

During one of their training missions they decided to test the limits of how long they could remain on the bottom without refreshing the air. Dixon's theory was that, if they successfully attacked a surface ship, they may need stay submerged for safety and a changing tide. They estimated that half an hour was the limit.

They flooded the ballast tanks, and the *Hunley* settled on the bottom. The crew then sat in total silence. Dixon, no doubt, sat quietly at the controls, rubbing the warp in the gold coin where the Yankee bullet had struck. The only illumination inside the submarine was a flickering candle, which snuffed itself out half an hour later. So the men sat in darkness – with time seeming to stand still - until all of them were light-headed from lack of oxygen. They then began to pump furiously and the bow started to rise. However, the stern remained on the bottom.

In complete darkness, working only by feel and his intimate familiarity with the machinery, Alexander discovered seaweed blocking the valve. He managed to clear the obstruction, pumped out the tanks and the *Hunley* bobbed to the surface. Dixon and Alexander threw open the hatches and the men gasped the fresh sea air.

They had been on the bottom two-and-a-half hours.

The experience convinced the crew to make a decision: if the boat became stuck beneath the surface again, they would flood the vessel and drown themselves. They preferred the quick death of drowning to the long, panicked agony of suffocation.

At the beginning of February, William Alexander was ordered back to Mobile by Gen. Beauregard to help build a rapid-fire repeating gun for the Confederate army. At this point in the War, the Confederacy relied on imports and needed to manufacture its own weapons.

On a cold, clear night, February 17, 1864, after two months of training the new crew, the *Hunley* left the wharf at Battery Marshall. After the tide turned, it silently sailed out of Breach Inlet, into the Atlantic Ocean and history. It headed for the Federal blockade, four miles offshore. Dixon was most likely dismayed that it was such a clear night. The *Hunley* would more easily visible as it approached its target, prior to diving.

The plan was simple: after the *Hunley* had accomplished its mission, it would surface and flash a blue phosphorus lamp. At that signal, the troops watching on Sullivan's Island would light a bonfire on the beach to guide it home.

The USS *Housatonic* was a 1,240-ton sloop-of-war launched November 20, 1861. Eighty-five feet wide, 205-feet long with a beam of thirty-eight feet, the *Housatonic*, with a crew of 155 men, had arrived in Charleston on September 11, 1862 and immediately took a position off the bar.

When the Union authorities had first learned of the *Hunley* and the *Davids* - and the real possibility of underwater attack - Admiral John A. Dahlgren wasted no time in laying out defensive plans. He ordered the ships to change anchorage regularly and keep guns trained on the water at all time. He also advised:

> ... not to anchor in the deepest part of the channel, for by not leaving much space between the bottom of the vessel and the bottom of the channel it will be impossible

for the diving torpedo to operate except on the side, and
there will be less difficulty in raising a vessel if sunk.

It would soon prove to be a prescient order.

At 8:40 P.M. black sailor, Robert F. Flemming, saw something
unusual floating in the moonlit water, about 400 feet away. He
reported the sighting to an officer, who, after looking, told him, "It's
a log."

Flemming responded, "It's not floating with the tide, like a log
would, it's moving across the tide."

At 8:45 P.M. John Crosby, the *Housatonics'* acting master, also
saw a glint of something in the moonlight "like a porpoise coming to
the surface to blow." It was about 100 yards off the starboard beam.
When he looked again, it was gone. He called out an order to "slip
the chain, back the engine."

A moment later an explosion of ninety pounds of gunpowder
rocked the warship. Water rushed into the engine room, smashing
timbers and metal, and the ship lurched to port and started to list.
Most of the men were asleep in their bunks, and dozens of them were
tossed into the ocean as an entire section of the ship disappeared.

Sailors on deck fired their rifles over the sides and soon found
themselves standing in water; the ship was sinking. Many of the crew
manned lifeboats and began to pick their mates out of the frigid
Atlantic water. Others simply climbed the ship's rigging to safety.

Within an hour of the explosion the *Housatonic* was sitting on the
bottom, in twenty-five feet of water, with only ten feet of the ship
above the waterline. Out of a crew of 155 there were only five
fatalities.

Robert F. Flemming, who first sited the "log," was one of those
hanging from the ship's rigging, waiting to be rescued. Off the
starboard bow he saw a blue light shine for a moment. Then, it was
gone. But he saw it.

On the beach at Sullivan's Island, after the blue light signaled,
the soldiers lit the bonfire and kept it burning until dawn, but the
Hunley never returned.

U.S.S. Housatonic – first ship to be sunk by a submarine attack.
Courtesy Library of Congress

The following day, Lt. Colonel O.M. Dantzler sent Beauregard a brief note:

> I have the honor to report that the torpedo-boat stationed at this point went out on the night of the 17th instant (Wednesday) and has not returned. The signals agreed upon to be given in case the boat wished a light to be exposed at this post as a guide for its return were observed and answered.

Over the next few days the story of the attack was pieced together. Beauregard sent a telegram to the Confederate command in Richmond:

> A gunboat sunken off Battery Marshall. Supposed to have been done by Mobile torpedo boat, under Lieutenant George E. Dixon, Company E, Twenty-first Alabama Volunteers, which went out for that purpose, and which I regret to say has not been heard of since ... There is little hope of the safety of that brave man and his associates, however, as they were not captured.

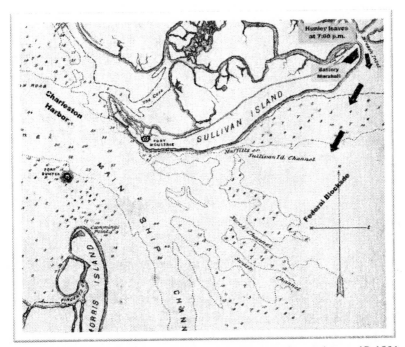

Map of Sullivan's Island Channel and the *Hunley's* likely path on February 17, 1864.
New labels by the author. Map *Courtesy Library of Congress*

The story of the successful attack was greeted with excitement across the South, positive news that was greatly needed for the southern psyche. On February 29, the *Charleston Daily Courier* reported:

> The glorious success of our little torpedo-boat, under the command of Lieutenant Dixon, of Mobile, has raised the hopes of our people, and the most sanguine expectations are now entertained of our being able to raise the siege in a way little dreamed of by the enemy.

The excitement was short-lived. On the first anniversary of the *Hunley* attack, February 17, 1865, Federal troops marched into Charleston. At the same time, 150 miles to the north, Columbia, the state capital, surrendered to Sherman's troops after being burned. For South Carolina, the War was over, but the story of the *Hunley* had another 140 years to reach its conclusion.

DISCOVERY & RECOVERY

As the years passed and countless histories of the War were written, through the mist of memory the *Hunley* became little more than a footnote, a factoid. In 1870 Jules Verne wrote *Twenty Leagues Under the Sea,* about the adventures of another submarine, the *Nautilus.*

Verne was obviously aware of the American Civil War. European newspapers covered the conflict in full and often sensational, detail. In 1865 Verne published a short story, "The Blockade Runners," in which a Scottish merchant captain uses a ship named the *Dolphin* to break the Union blockade of Charleston harbor.

In 1872-73, former Confederate diver, Angus Smith, who lived on Sullivan's Island, was given a contract to remove old wrecks from the channel. Smith was a member of the dive team that had raised the *Hunley* both times it had sunk. He was intimately familiar with the boat.

A couple of years later, Smith responded to a request for his memories about the torpedo boat from former General P.G.T. Beauregard, who was putting together his memoirs about the War. Smith claimed to have attempted a salvage of the *Hunley.* He wrote to Beauregard:

> I went to work to save the torpedo boat, and I got on top of her, and found out the cause of her sinking. The boat is outside or alongside the *Housatonic.* She can lifted any time our people wish ... she can be saved and my opinion is she is as good as the day she was sunk.

In all likelihood, that was the last sighting of the *Hunley* for more than 125 years.

Marker on Sullivan's Island, with Breach Inlet in the background.
Photo by author.

Sometime in the late 1870s, P.T. Barnum, master showman and businessman, offered a $100,000 reward to anyone who could salvage the *Hunley* for his traveling show of oddities. The staggering amount of money sparked off a round of searches and explorations that yielded nothing.

About the same time, the government began the construction of the stone jetties off the coast of Sullivan's Island – four-mile long groins designed to prevent the flow of sand from filling the main channel into Charleston harbor. Not only did the jetties alter sand flow, they changed the contour of Sullivan's Island and eroded most of Morris Island. They also slowly, but inevitably, buried the *Hunley* deeper.

In 1970, Charleston-based professional diver, Edward Lee Spence, dove off the side of a fishing boat in twenty-seven feet of water, attempting to free the line of a fish trap for his friend. Spence, a Civil War naval history expert, was intimately familiar with the thousands of wrecks up and down the Charleston coast. As he went over into the cold November water, he also knew he was close to the site of the *Housatonic.*

Along the bottom he found where the line was snagged on something that resembled a ledge. Upon closer examination, it was a solid black iron tube, about twenty-feet long, with the rest of it buried beneath the sand. In a flash, he realized what he was touching.

A moment later Spence surfaced and screamed out to his friends on the boat, "The *Hunley!* I've found the *Hunley!*" He tossed a buoy and, for claim purposes, he drew a crude map in an effort to mark the location. For the next twenty years, Spence crusaded to anyone who would listen about his discovery. The problem was: he could never find it again. He had no proof and refused to release its location, for looting purposes.

In 1994, two groups combined forces in an effort to find the *Hunley.* The South Carolina Institute of Archeology and Anthropology (SCIAA) issued all permits for anything excavated from South Carolina waters. Employee Mark Newell was an experienced diver and Civil War buff. His days off were often spent diving off the Charleston coast, mostly around the *Housatonic* site, searching for the *Hunley.* He agreed to a joint venture with a non-profit business, the National Underwater and Marine Agency (NUMA), operated by best-selling novelist, Clive Cussler. It was a bit of real life emulating fiction.

Cussler's fictional character, Dirk Pitt, is kind of a maritime James Bond. Pitt, who works for an organization called NUMA, first appeared in the 1973 novel *The Mediterranean Caper.* However, it was the third Pitt novel, *Raise The Titanic,* which vaulted Cussler to megaselling status, making him a wealthy man with more than forty million books sold.

This wealth made it possible for Cussler to establish a real-life version of NUMA to search for lost maritime treasures across the world. NUMA had great success, discovering more than sixty vessels. Cussler, however, vowed that before his death, he would find the *Hunley.*

Unfortunately, the joint NUMA/SCIAA mission was unsuccessful; it was marked with animosity and ended with no love lost between the two groups. However, the NUMA team continued the quest. Financed by Cussler, Ralph Wilbanks, Wes Hall and Harry Pecorilli continued a search for the *Hunley*. Periodically, Cussler would fax them new charts with newly marked locations to search, but after a dozen or so dives, their confidence was flagging. Cussler kept telling them "the damn things are never where they're supposed to be."

On May 3, 1995, Hall and Pecorilli dove a site they had mapped and explored earlier. During the earlier dive, the floor had been covered by a bed of oyster shells, but this time it was clear. Pecorilli began his exploration, poking a stainless steel probe into the sand when he made contact with a solid object. Using the vacuum hose, he cleared an area three-feet wide, while Hall explored the surface of the metal with his hand. Suddenly, he grabbed Pecorilli's arm and began to gesture. The two men surfaced a few minutes. Wilbanks, on board, looked down at them in the water. Hall said, "It's the Hunley."

A week later, May 11, Clive Cussler met with the media in front of the *Hunley* replica outside the Charleston museum. He played a videotape that the divers had made of their discovery. When asked for the coordinates he refused. He remarked:

> I didn't spend fifteen years looking for it only to have it broken up by amateurs. Until I see a comprehensive plan put together by qualified people, they won't get any cooperation from me.

Within days, South Carolina was in another skirmish with the United States government: legal ownership of the *Hunley*. Under the rules of war, the United States government owned all Confederate vessels. So, technically, it was the property of the Navy, and the General Services Administration would make the decision.

State Senator Glenn McConnell, from Charleston, rushed a resolution through the legislature asking the U.S. Congress to give South Carolina title to the vessel. U.S. Congressman Mark Sanford, also from Charleston, quickly registered a bill to that effect, followed almost immediately by Alabama. Both southern states had good claims: it was constructed in one state, and lost in the other. They were also fearful that the Smithsonian Institution would use its formidable power and claim the *Hunley* for its collections.

South Carolina then fired a shot across the bow of the federal government's claim. McConnell, at this time was chairman of the hastily formed *Hunley* Commission, claimed that the U.S. government had no claim, since the *Hunley* was never a Confederate vessel – it was a privateer, designed and built with private money. *Hunley* commission lawyers produced papers from Horace Hunley's business concerns that proved McConnell's supposition. The lawyers argued that, according to South Carolina state law, any private property that was abandoned for more than a year and a day, the rights were forfeited.

They also argued that Federal jurisdiction only extended three miles into the ocean. Since the *Hunley* was almost four miles from shore, it did not fall under Federal purview.

Finally, an agreement was struck: The U.S. government kept title to the *Hunley*, and the submarine would stay in Charleston. The SCIAA, National Park Service and the Naval Historical Center were to be involved in the recovery of the submarine and the *Hunley* Commission was appointed to direct and manage the display of the vessel.

Cussler gave up his coordinates and within the year, a platoon of divers/archeologists from all the agencies verified the claim: it was the *Hunley*.

Five years later, August 8, 2000, the *H.L. Hunley* broke the surface of the Atlantic Ocean for the first time in 136 years. With hundreds of boats dotting the surface, carrying thousands of onlookers, the *Hunley* raising was broadcast to the world.

Thousands of people in Charleston, and from all across the South, ditched work and found some location to watch the historic event. Hanging from its secure sling, the *Hunley* and a flotilla of hundreds of boats sailed into Charleston harbor, past Fort Sumter, past Castle Pinkney, and up the Cooper River. More than 20,000 people lined Charleston's Battery sea wall, beaches, parks and marinas to view the submarine's procession.

As the parade approached the U.S.S. *Yorktown,* a World War II aircraft carrier and part of a permanent museum on the Cooper River, a regiment of Confederate reenactors fired a twenty-one gun salute from the deck. A lamp on the carrier was lit with a blue light, signaling "Mission Accomplished," one-hundred and thirty-six years later.

The submarine was placed in a deep water tank at the former Charleston Navy base. The next steps were her conservation and her excavation.

In March 2001 chief archaeologist Maria Jacobson became the first person to fully enter the submarine. As she cleared away the thick muddy sediment that filled the iron tube, she came across the remains of the first crewman. Over the next few weeks six more sets of remains were discovered. It was hoped that the remains of George Dixon, would be found in the forward conning tower.

Meanwhile, in addition to the careful extraction of the bodies, a steady stream of artifacts daily – pipes, clothing, buttons and pocketknives – was being recovered almost on a daily basis as the submarine slowly reveled her secrets.

On May 17, 2001, the archaeologists discovered a signal lamp in the conning tower - and also, the remains of Lt. George E. Dixon. Five days later, as Maria Jacobson was working on preparing Dixon's body for removal, her fingers ran across a small, solid circular object near the pelvis. She held the object in her muddy hand and as water poured over it, a warped gold coin was revealed. She turned it over, and read the inscription "Shiloh. April 6th 1862. My life Preserver. G.E.D."

The recovery of the lost submarine and crew was a remarkable feat, involving equal parts luck and human perseverance and endeavor. But the discovery of Dixon's coin was even more unlikely: legend became fact.

The last funeral of the War Between the States fittingly took place in Charleston on April 17, 2004. The third crew of the *Hunley* took its final voyage, a four-and-a-half mile journey from White Point Garden in downtown Charleston to Magnolia Cemetery. More than 400 journalists from around the world covered the event. Ten-thousand reenactors participated, and more than 50,000 people lined the streets to watch the procession pass.

After a memorial ceremony at 9:15 A.M., horse-drawn caissons carried the crew down East Bay Street to Magnolia Cemetery, where they were interred next to the first two *Hunley* crews.

IN MEMORIUM

H.L. Hunley

FIRST CREW: AUGUST 29th, 1863
Michael Cane
Nicholas Davis
Frank Doyle
John Kelly
Absolum Williams

SECOND CREW: OCTOBER 15, 1863
Horace Hunley - captain
Robert Brockbank
Joseph Patterson
Thomas W. Park
Charles McHugh
Henry Beard
John Marshall
Charles L. Sprague

THIRD CREW: FEBRUARY 17, 1864
Lieutenant George E. Dixon
Arnold Becker
F.F. Carlsen
Frank Collins
James A. Wicks
Joseph Ridgaway
C. Lumpkin
Miller

36 1865 FIRST MEMORIAL DAY

A number of towns around the nation lay claim to holding the first Memorial Day. The distinction generally goes to the town of Waterloo, New York. However, not so fast. Charleston has a claim too.

On May 1, 1865, more than 10,000 people marched in a parade, heard speeches and dedicated the graves of Union dead at what is now Hampton Park in Charleston. The group consisted of several thousand black freedmen, northern missionaries and teachers. The Northerners had moved to Charleston to teach the newly emancipated black population.

Hampton Park was originally the Planters Race Course and, during the final months of the Civil War, it became a hellish open-air Confederate prison. A total of 257 Union soldiers died there, some of whom had been transferred from infamously horrific Andersonville in Georgia, before its liberation.

The dead were originally buried by the Confederates in an unmarked, hastily-dug mass grave. In April 1865, twenty-eight members of local black churches reburied the soldiers in individual graves at the site. They built a fence around the cemetery with an arch over the entrance which read "The Martyrs of the Race Course."

On May Day, 1865 a large assembly marched to the burial site. Nearly everyone brought flowers to place on the burial field. A *New York Tribune* correspondent witnessed the event, described as "a procession of friends and mourners as South Carolina and the United States never saw before."

TOP: Grandstands and clubhouse of the Planters Race Course, where Union soldiers were imprisoned. BOTTOM: Burial site of soldiers on the race course.
Courtesy Library of Congress

David Blight, a history professor at Yale, wrote about the event:

> The symbolic power of the low-country planter aristocracy's horse track (where they had displayed their wealth, leisure, and influence) was not lost on the freed people.

The procession began at 9:00 A.M., led by 3,000 black children carrying roses and singing "John Brown's Body." They were followed by several hundred black women with baskets of flowers and crosses. Black men marched in cadence next, followed by Union soldiers, including the famous 54th Massachusetts (depicted in the movie *Glory*), the 34th and 104th U.S. Colored Troops.

Inside the cemetery a children's choir sang several spirituals, "We'll Rally Around the Flag" and "The Star Spangled Banner." Several black ministers read Bible scriptures. After the service, the crowd gathered for a picnic, watched the soldiers drill and listened to speeches.

They called it Decoration Day, an annual ritual of remembrance. David Blight wrote:

> This was the first Memorial Day. African Americans invented Memorial Day in Charleston, South Carolina. What you have there is black Americans recently freed from slavery announcing to the world with their flowers, their feet, and their songs what the war had been about. What they basically were creating was the Independence Day of a Second American Revolution.

In 1876 former Confederate General Wade Hampton declared that it was time for white Southerners to "dedicate themselves to the redemption of the South." Hampton was elected South Carolina governor that year in one of the most volatile elections in state history, filled with riots, murders, intimidations and blatant voter fraud.

Hampton narrowly defeated Republican Governor Daniel Chamberlain, despite the presence of Federal troops under General William T. Sherman attempting to stop violent mob action at the polls. On election night, the voter count in Laurens and Edgefield counties exceeded the total population, with most of the votes going to Hampton and the Democrats.

Hampton won the election by less than 1,200 votes and each side claimed victory, accusing the other of fraud. To make matters worse, the Democrats won control of the House and the Republicans won the Senate. Both parties moved into the State House and refused to leave, sleeping on the floor and attempting to conduct legislative business. Outside, supporters of each side gathered as police and militia tried to keep the crowds from turning into mobs.

After the South Carolina Supreme Court ruled in favor of the Republicans (see #37), Chamberlain, with the support of Federal troops, was inaugurated as the governor on December 6, 1876. Hampton claimed that "the people of South Carolina have elected me Governor, and by the Eternal God, I will be the Governor!"

For the next four months South Carolina had rival houses and governors, each claiming to be the legitimate government. White citizens refused to pay their taxes to the Republican administration, but voluntarily contributed ten percent to the Democrat government. If a state agency wanted money to operate, they had to ask Hampton for funds. Soon there were defections from the Republican administration and Chamberlain's power base eroded.

When Rutherford B. Hayes was inaugurated as the President of the United States, both governors appeared before him. Hayes announced that "the whole army of United States would be inadequate to enforce the authority of Governor Chamberlain." He ordered the evacuation of the Federal troops from South Carolina and in the first week of April 1877, Chamberlain and the Republicans vacated their offices.

Despite the chaos, the election accomplished Hampton's goal, wrenching control from post-War Republicans, many from the North, and returning it back into the hands of the white Democrats. The Democrats began to institute a series of laws and reforms that removed tens of thousands of blacks from voter rolls. They also established a Confederate Memorial Day, designed to help smother the memory of the annual Decoration Day for fallen Union soldiers.

David Blight wrote about the loss of Decoration Day:

As the Lost Cause tradition set in — the Confederate version of the meaning and memory of the war — no one in white Charleston or the state was interested in remembering the war through this event.

By this time the race course cemetery was suffering from neglect, and the soldiers' remains were reinterred at the Beaufort and Florence National Cemeteries. In 1902 the site of the race course and former cemetery became part of the fairgrounds for the South Carolina Inter-State and West Indian Exposition. At the conclusion of the Expo, the city of Charleston acquired the land for a park, which they ironically named in honor of General and Governor Wade Hampton.

Hampton Park, circa 1906. *Courtesy Library of Congress*

Through the years Memorial Day has generally been celebrated on May 30. Beginning in 1971, however, the last Monday in May was designated at the federal holiday.

Marker honoring the first Memorial Day and Union cemetery. *Photo by author*

37 1870   FIRST BLACK ASSOCIATE JUSTICE OF A STATE SUPREME COURT

In 1840, Jonathan Jasper Wright was born in Pennsylvania. He attended the district school during the winter months and worked for neighboring farmers the rest of the year. He saved up enough money to attend Lancasterian University in Ithaca, New York.

Wright graduated in 1860 and for the next five years taught school and read law in Pennsylvania. In October 1864 Wright was a delegate to the National Convention of Colored Men in Syracuse, NY. Chaired by Frederick Douglass, the convention called for a nationwide ban on slavery, racial equality under the law and suffrage for all males.

Wright then applied for admission to the Pennsylvania Bar but was refused due to his race. After the War he joined the American Missionary Association and was sent to Beaufort, South Carolina to organize schools for freedmen.

When the Civil Rights Act was passed, Wright returned to Pennsylvania and demanded a Bar examination. He was admitted on August 13, 1865, and became the state's first black lawyer. By January 1867 he was back in South Carolina as head of the Freedmen's Bureau in Beaufort where he became active in Republican politics. He was chosen as a delegate to the historic 1868 South Carolina Constitutional Convention that met in Charleston. As one of the few trained black lawyers in South Carolina, Wright had a great deal of influence in writing the Constitution and setting up the judiciary.

In a somewhat back-handed compliment, the Charleston *Daily News* called Wright a "very intelligent, well-spoken colored lawyer."

There were 124 delegates to the convention, seventy-three of them black. The new Constitution bestowed voting rights and educational opportunities "without regard to race or color." It also included universal male suffrage, forbade all property qualifications for office, outlawed dueling and legalized divorce.

Later that year, in the first election under this new Constitution, Wright was one of ten black men elected to the South Carolina Senate. In the South Carolina House seventy-eight of the 124 representatives were black. However, many whites had no intention of "obeying a Negro constitution of a Negro government establishing Negro equality." The white-dominated press called it the "Africanization of South Carolina," and most whites never accepted the 1868 Constitution as legitimate. They were determined to undermine all the gains made by blacks with the support of Yankee carpetbaggers.

Shortly after the election, Solomon Hogue resigned from the South Carolina Supreme Court to take a seat in the U.S. Congress. That left a vacant seat on the high court for the ten-month remainder of his judicial term,. The black Republican-dominated legislature was determined to elect a black man to join the two white men - Chief Justice Franklin J. Moses, a scalawag (Southerner who supported the Federal government), and Associate Justice A.J. Willard, a carpetbagger (Yankee involved in Southern politics) – already on the court.

In fact, Moses, a former governor, who was notoriously corrupt, picked up the nickname "king of the scalawags" and "the Robber Governor."

The three candidates for the open seat were Wright, J.W. Whipper, a black representative, and one white candidate, former governor James Orr. The final legislative vote on February 1, 1870 was:

* Wright, 72
* Whipper, 57
* Orr, 3

Jonathan Jasper Wright became the first black associate justice elected to a state Supreme Court. Ten months later, Wright was elected to a full term (six years). He was thirty-years-old.

Jonathan Jasper Wright, from *Harper's* magazine. *Author's collection.*

Edward McCrady of Charleston was incensed by Wright's election to the high court. He published a virulent pamphlet which claimed that had Wright been a white man, he never would have attained such a position with so little experience.

During his seven-year tenure on the bench, Justice Wright heard 425 cases and wrote eighty-seven opinions. However, during the heated election of 1876 (see entry #36), Wright voted to support the

Republican victory against Democrat Wade Hampton. Four months later when President Rutherford B. Hayes pulled Federal troops out of South Carolina, the Republicans vacated their seats and the Democrats took charge of the state.

The new Democrat-controlled legislature quickly attempted to impeach Justice Wright for corruption and malfeasance based on trumped-up charges. He initially vowed to defend himself, but in August 1877 realized he could not win. He submitted his resignation.

Governor Hampton, in accepting the resignation, wrote to Wright, acknowledging the illegitimacy of the accusations:

> Dear Sir:
>
> Your favor of this date, covering your resignation of the office of Associate Justice of the Supreme Court of this State, is at hand and contents noted.
>
> I accept the same as a tribute on your part to the quietude of the State, and as in no sense an acknowledgement of the truth of the charges which have been made against you.

Wright moved to Charleston and established a law practice. He taught classes from his office and established the law department at Claflin College in Orangeburg. When he died of tuberculosis in 1885, his reputation in South Carolina was still viewed through the lens of racism and suspicion.

A century later, in 1997, the South Carolina Supreme Court unveiled a portrait of Wright, originally published in *Harper's Weekly* magazine and a granite grave marker. Chief Justice Ernest Finney, Jr., the first black on the court since Wright stated:

> [Wright's] election to the supreme court marked a high point in a celebrated career of public service, as a teacher, a lawyer and as a statesman.

On Thursday, September 26, 2013, at the South Carolina Black Lawyers Association hosted a ceremonial unveiling of a South Carolina Historic Marker at the site of Justice Jonathan Jasper Wright's law office on Queen Street in Charleston.

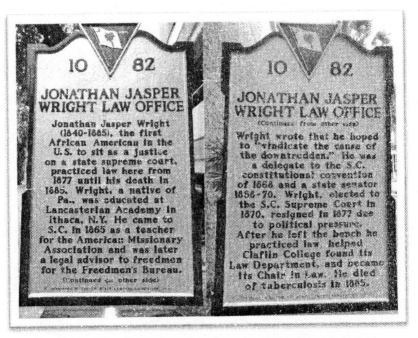

Historic marker on Queen Street for Jonathan Wright. *Photo by author*

38 1931 FIRST MUNICIPAL HISTORICAL ZONING ORDINANCE

October 13, 1931.

Charleston City Council approved a Historic Preservation Ordinance and established the Board of Architectural Review. The ordinance stated its purpose.

> In order to promote general welfare through the preservation and protection of the old historic or architecturally worthy structures and quaint neighborhoods which impart a distinct aspect to the city and which serve as visible reminders of the historical and cultural heritage of the city, the state and the nation.

For the first time in an American city, buildings were designated as significant and worthy of protection. The blending of planning and preservation was considered a unique idea at the time, but in reality passing of the ordinance was merely an official recognition of a long-standing community attitude.

Visitors to Charleston often hear that due to the economic stress of the post-Civil War era the locals were "too poor to paint and too proud to whitewash." Like many a pithy expression, it is an oversimplification that glosses over a deeper story: Charlestonians have long taken pride in their city's visual appeal.

In 1835, when members of St. Philip's Church were rebuilding their edifice after losing the previous one in a fire they argued against erecting modern buildings "in favour of the old public buildings."

An 1857 article in *Harper's Weekly* stated:

> There are two Charlestons; the old and the new ... The old is formidable in sheer stubbornness and ... very

immovable [and] spend a great deal of money furbishing up the old.

Arthur Mazyck wrote a Charleston guidebook in 1875. It is infused with a romantic golden-haze-of-memory aura that has become associated with Charleston's preservation movement.

> Beautiful as a dream, tinged with romance, consecrated by tradition, glorified by history, rising from the very bosom of the waves, like a fairy city created by the enchanter's wand ... that was, and is, Charleston, thanks to her people's preservation ethic.

In 1902 the Charleston committee of the National Society of the Colonial Dames in the State of South Carolina purchased the Powder Magazine from the Manigault family for $1000. Constructed in 1713 for gunpowder storage, the Magazine is the oldest public structure in South Carolina.

In 1913, after extreme lobbying, Congress deeded the Old Exchange building to the state Daughters of the American Revolution Completed in 1771, the Exchange is considered to be one of colonial America's most important public buildings. It has hosted many historic events that include the state U.S. Constitution Ratification Convention and several receptions and entertainments for President George Washington.

In 1920 local Charleston real estate agent Susan Pringle Frost founded the Society for the Preservation of Old Dwellings, today known as the Preservation Society of Charleston. The Society purchased the Joseph Manigault House to save it from demolition. It was later purchased by the Charleston Museum.

Today the Powder Magazine, the Exchange Building and the Manigault House are National Historic Landmarks and operate as museums, enjoyed by tens of thousands of visitors annually. They were the guideposts for future preservation efforts in Charleston.

The Society then purchased six dilapidated buildings on East Bay Street between Tradd and Elliott streets. Consisting of pre-and post-Revolutionary commercial buildings on the Charleston water-front, which had deteriorated into slums. Frost did not have the money for restoration, but purchased them to prevent demolition.

Joseph Manigault House. *Courtesy Library of Congress.*

Dorothy Porcher Legge purchased 99-101 East Bay from Susan Frost in 1931 and renovated them. She chose to paint the houses pink based on Charleston's colonial Caribbean heritage. Through the years as the rest of the buildings on this East Bay Street block were refurbished, other owners continued the pastel color scheme. By the end of World War II they had created one of Charleston's most photographed landmarks: Rainbow Row.

In 1929 Charleston's Special Committee on Zoning hired Morris Knowles, a planning consultant from Pittsburgh. With the assistance of local architect Albert Simons, Knowles conducted a survey of important 18th-century buildings in the oldest part of the city. On

October 13, 1931, Charleston City Council ratified the proposed historic district zoning ordinance.

Rainbow Row, circa 1900, looking north from South Adger's Wharf.
Courtesy Library of Congress

During the Depression, the city utilized some available federal funds for preservation purposes and in 1939 the city razed a number of dilapidated buildings outside the historic district as defined by the 1931 ordinance.

In 1959 Historic Charleston Foundation targeted the Ansonborough neighborhood for rehabilitation. Once one of Charleston's grandest neighborhoods, during the early part of the 20th century the area descended into disarray and neglect. The Foundation developed a program of purchase-and-resale for the neighborhood. A revolving fund was established to purchase structures for restoration, and when sold, that money was used to purchase and restore other properties. It was an outstanding success. Today, Ansonborough has been returned to its former glory and one of Charleston's most architecturally intact neighborhoods.

Also in 1959 the City Council revised the historic zoning ordinance for the first time. It granted the Board of Architectural Review authority over proposed demolitions and the review of exterior alterations to any pre-1860 structures, as well as to any buildings within the Old and Historic Charleston district. In 1974 the city instituted a pioneering Historic Preservation Plan, which specifically outlined measures to protect Charleston's historic and architectural heritage.

During the beginning of the 21st century, Charleston became the #1 tourist city in America, and its strict preservation laws are an important part of the allure. Today, when the six million annual visitors to Charleston wander up and down the narrow streets, they literally are immersed in history, strolling through a living, breathing museum that is home to more than 35,000 proud souls.

39 1935   FIRST AMERICAN "FOLK" OPERA

Stephen Sondheim in *Invisible Giants: Fifty Americans Who Shaped the Nation But Missed the History Books*, wrote:

> DuBose Heyward has gone largely unrecognized as the author of the finest set of lyrics in the history of the American musical theater - namely, those of *Porgy and Bess*. There are two reasons for this, and they are connected. First, he was primarily a poet and novelist, and his only song lyrics were those that he wrote for *Porgy*. Second, some of them were written in collaboration with Ira Gershwin, a full-time lyricist, whose reputation in the musical theater was firmly established before the opera was written. But most of the lyrics in *Porgy* - and all of the distinguished ones - are by Heyward. I admire his theater songs for their deeply felt poetic style and their insight into character. It's a pity he didn't write any others. His work is sung, but he is unsung.

In 1922 a petition was sent to Charleston City Council, signed by thirty-seven white residents of Church Street and St. Michael's Alley, which called for the immediate eviction of all the black residents of Cabbage Row. The petition detailed their unsavory behavior which included fornication between of black women and white sailors, knife and gun fights, unsanitary conditions and "the most vile, filthy and offensive language."

During the spring of 1924, DuBose Heyward, founding member of the Poetry Society of South Carolina, began to work on "a novel of contemporary Charleston." Heyward was the descendant of

Thomas Heyward Jr., a signer of the Declaration of Independence. He was part of Charleston's aristocratic heritage where family bloodlines were more important than bank accounts.

During the early 1920s DuBose Heyward gained a reputation in American literary circles as a talented, serious poet. Charleston society was rightly proud of his success and reputation. The perception at Charleston tea parties was that his forthcoming novel of "contemporary Charleston" would, of course, be a drawing room drama, or a comedy of manners. Everyone was anxious to read it, assuming it would be about "them." They could have never imagined what Heyward actually wrote, a lyrical folk novel about the Gullahs of Charleston.

For many white Charlestonians, the ubiquitous presence of Gullahs was as common as the humidity, present but rarely acknowledged. Heyward lived on Church Street, a dignified colonial-era neighborhood that had become quite ungentrified after Emancipation. Whites descended from the elite families of Charleston society now lived in close quarters, side-by-side, with descendants of their former slaves. The once pristine houses and gardens were now covered in shabbiness, the result of decades of dwindling fortunes and cultural depression.

Heyward became fascinated by the odd story of Samuel Smalls. The Charleston *News and Courier* featured a small item on the police blotter:

> Samuel Smalls, who is a cripple and is familiar to King Street, with his goat and cart, was held for the June term of Court of Sessions on an aggravated assault charge. It is alleged that on Saturday night he attempted to shoot Maggie Barnes at number four Romney Street. His shots went wide of the mark. Smalls was up on a similar charge some months ago and was given a suspended sentence. Smalls had attempted to escape in his wagon and was run down and captured by the police guard.

Heyward finished the first draft of a novel based on Smalls's life. He gave the manuscript to his friend John Bennett to read. Bennett was astonished by the story. "There had never been anything like it," he said.

The story was set in a location Heyward called "Catfish Row," two run-down tenement buildings one block from his home on Church Street. Nestled between the two tenements was 87 Church Street, a classic brick Georgian double house that had been the home of his ancestor, Thomas Heyward, Jr. As previously noted, by the turn of the 20th century both tenements were notorious as dens of crime and violence.

85-91 Church Street, circa 1910. These pre-Revolutionary structures had deteriorated into slums by the 1920s. (L-R) Cabbage Row, Thomas Heyward Jr. House and Cabbage Row. *Courtesy of the Library of Congress*

DuBose Heyward's novel, published in September 1925, was titled *Porgy*. It was the story of a crippled beggar on the streets of Charleston. During a dice game, Porgy witnesses a murder committed by a rough, sadistic black man named Crown, who runs away from the police. During the next weeks, Porgy shelters the murderer's woman, the haunted Bess, in the rear courtyard of Catfish Row, a rundown tenement on the Charleston waterfront. Porgy and Bess fall in love. However, when Crown arrives to take Bess back Porgy kills him. He is taken in by police for questioning. After ten days he is released, because the police do not believe a crippled beggar could have killed the powerful Crown. When Porgy returns to the Row, he discovers that Bess had fallen under the spell of the drug dealer Sportin' Life and his "happy dus'." She has followed Sportin' Life to a new future in Savannah and Porgy is left alone, brokenhearted.

The novel became a national best-seller, and received rave reviews. DuBose Heyward was praised for portraying "Negro life more colorful and spirited and vital than that of the white community" and for creating a character that is "a real Negro, not a black-faced white man," who "thinks as a Negro, feels as a Negro, lives as a Negro."

In Charleston, the reaction was polite but less positive. Some acknowledged the truth: it was a powerful book. Others claimed "the paper was wasted on which it was writ." Most people were disappointed and shocked, when they discovered *Porgy's* main characters were black, not white. The white characters were little more than poorly drawn caricatures.

Lost amidst the initial praise and criticism, that, at its heart, *Porgy,* is a reminiscence of the old way of life in Charleston. Blacks are second class citizens, living lives of limited freedom and still expected to be subservient to whites. *Porgy,* however, examines this world from a black viewpoint. Portrayed with realism, these Charleston blacks were far removed from the "new Negro," who could be seen daily on the streets of Harlem, and appearing in the literature of New York writers. In Charleston blacks and whites suffered from the same malaise.

In 1924 George Gershwin's musical, *Lady Be Good!* ran for 330 performances on Broadway, establishing him as one of the most popular songwriters in America. While his second hit show, *Tip-Toes*, was on Broadway, Gershwin read *Porgy* in one sitting. He immediately wrote to Heyward proposing the two men collaborate together on an opera based on the story.

Heyward was astonished, and then excited. Gershwin was one of the most powerful, successful and talented artists in the New York musical world. He contacted Gershwin and was told that, although the composer wanted to create an opera his work schedule was booked solid for the next several years. Heyward decided to go ahead and write a nonmusical stage version of *Porgy*.

DuBose Heyward's wife, Dorothy, was an award-winning

playwright. The two had met in 1922 at the MacDowell Colony, an artist retreat in New Hampshire, and Heyward was immediately smitten. In 1923 they married in New York where Dorothy's play, *Nancy Ann,* won Harvard's Belmont Prize, beating out Thomas Wolfe's *Welcome to My City.* First prize was $500 and a Broadway production of the play. Meanwhile, MacMillan Publishing had accepted a volume of Heyward's poetry for publication. The young couple spent the first months of their marriage living apart, Dorothy in New York working on the play production and Heyward on a speaking tour across the South.

Heyward's decision to go ahead with a dramatic stage version of *Porgy,* instead of waiting for Gershwin, was an important one. After all, he already had the perfect collaborator living under the same roof. Together the Heywards turned the novel into a stage play. Gershwin was fully supportive of the effort. He told Heyward that a stage script of the story could more easily be transformed into a libretto for the proposed opera.

Dorothy wrote most of the dialogue for the play, smoothing the Gullah dialect from the novel into more recognizable English. By the summer of 1926 the play was written and submitted to three professional production companies in New York. One week later, it was accepted by the Theatre Guild, but the Heywards were pessimistic that the play would ever be produced. They had one unshakable demand, which could easily have been the death knell of the production; they wanted black actors to play the black roles, not white actors in blackface, still common at the time. The original director resigned due to their demands and the play was set aside.

In early 1927 a young Armenian director named Rouben Mamoulian decided he would direct *Porgy,* with a black cast. Trained as a lawyer, Mamoulian and his sister had fled Russia during the Bolshevik Revolution, moved to London and began working in West End theaters. Mamoulian arrived in America at the invitation of George Eastman (of Eastman-Kodak) to work for the American Opera Company. It was there that he attracted the attention of the Theatre Guild, who asked him to stage *Porgy.*

Over the next thirty years, Mamoulian came to be known as "the mad Armenian" due to his frenetic energy. He directed more than twenty Hollywood movies and several successful Broadway plays, including the original *Oklahoma* (1943) and *Carousel* (1945). *Porgy*, however, was to be his first opportunity in charge of a Broadway production.

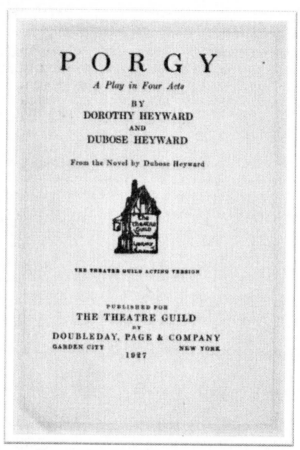

Cover of script for *Porgy*, the play. *Author's Collection*

To prepare, Mamoulian traveled to Charleston to soak up the atmosphere and learn about the Gullah culture. On his second day in Charleston, he was taken to the Jenkins Orphanage for an after-dinner private concert. Several women sang spirituals and then members of the Jenkins Band performed. Mamoulian was amazed by the band's "melodious discordance" and the "infinitesimally small darkey boy who led the band." Before leaving Charleston the next day, he persuaded Rev. Daniel Jenkins to allow the band to appear in the *Porgy* production.

Opening night for *Porgy* was October 10, 1927. At the beginning of the second act, when the cast travels to Kittawah Island for the picnic, they were led onstage by the Jenkins Band playing "Sons and Daughters Repent Ye Saith the Lord."

Within a week, *Porgy* was playing to standing-room-only audiences. When it closed after 367 performances it was viewed as an overwhelming success, with a higher box office than its main competitor, Eugene O'Neill's *All God's Chillun Got Wings*. During its run *Porgy* employed more than sixty black performers in a serious drama, unheard of on Broadway at that time.

Five years later, George Gershwin's heavy work schedule finally lightened enough to allow him to devote his energies to the opera. In late February 1934 he reported to Heyward that "I have begun composing music for the first act, and I am starting with the songs and spirituals first." He then asked Heyward to join him in New York so the work could be expedited. Over the next two months, while living in a guest suite at Gershwin's famous fourteen-room house at 132 East Seventy-second Street, Heyward wrote the lyrics for almost a dozen Gershwin compositions, including "Summertime," "A Woman Is a Sometime Thing," "Buzzard Song," "It Take A Long Pull to Get There," "My Man's Gone," "It Ain't Necessarily So" and "I Got Plenty of Nuttin'." The opera was beginning to take shape.

In June 1934, George Gershwin arrived by train in Charleston with his cousin, artist Henry Botkin. They drove out to Folly Beach, where Heyward had rented a cottage at 708 West Arctic Avenue.

Folly Beach was a remote, sparsely developed barrier island ten miles from Charleston. It was a vastly different world from Gershwin's New York neighborhood, in the middle of rollicking night life and luxurious accommodations. Life at Folly Beach was at best simple and at worst primitive. The surrounding marshes were filled with gators and other wild, exotic creatures. Crabs and snakes entered houses freely. Heat and humidity often reached equatorial proportions. In his letters Gershwin complained that the heat "brought out the flys, and knats, and mosquitos," leaving "nothing to do but scratch." Two weeks later, the *Herald-Journal* (Spartanburg,

S.C.) filed this story:

GERSHWIN, GONE NATIVE, BASKS AT FOLLY BEACH
Charleston, June 30.

Bare and black above the waist, an inch of hair bristling from his face, and with a pair of tattered knickers furnishing a sole connected link with civilization, George Gershwin, composer of jazz music, had gone native. He is staying at the Charles T. Tamsberg cottage at Folly Beach, South Carolina.

"I have become acclimated," he said yesterday as he ran his hand experimentally through a crop of dark, matted hair which had not had the benefit of being combed for many, many days. "You know, it's so pleasant here that it's really a shame to work."

Two weeks at Folly have made a different Gershwin from the almost sleek creator of "Rhapsody in Blue" and "Concerto in F" who arrived from New York City on June 16. Naturally brown, he is now black. Naturally sturdy, he is now sturdier. Gershwin, it would seem intends to play the part of Crown, the tremendous buck in "Porgy" who lunges a knife into the throat of a friend too lucky at craps and who makes women love him by placing huge black hands about their throats and tensing their muscles.

The opera "Porgy" which Gershwin is writing from the book and play by DuBose Heyward, is to be a serious musical work to be presented by the Guild Theater early next year, is an interpretation in sound of the life in Charleston' "Catfish Row"; an impressionistic dissertation on the philosophy of negro life and the relationship between the negro and the white. Mr. Heyward, who is staying at Lester Karow's cottage at the beach, spends every afternoon with the composer, cutting the score, rewriting and whipping the now-completed first act into final form.

"We are attempting to have an opera that is serious and dramatic," Mr. Gershwin said. "The whites will speak their lines, but the negroes will sing throughout. I hope the audience will get the idea. With the colored people there is always a song, see? They always find something to sing about somewhere. The whites are dull and drab."

It is the crap game scene and subsequent murder by Crown which may make the first act the most dramatic of the production. A strange rhythm and an acid, biting quality in the music create the sensation of conflict and strife between men and strife caused by the rolling bones of luck.

"You won't hear the dice click and roll," he said. "It is impressionism, not realism. When you want to get a great painting of nature you don't take a camera with you."

Jazz will rear its hotcha head at intervals through the more serious music. Sporting Life, the negro who peddles "joy powder" or dope, to the residents of Catfish Row, will be represented by ragtime.

"Even though we are cutting as much as possible, it is going to be a very long opera," Mr. Gershwin said. "It takes three times as long to sing a line as it does to say it. In the first act, scene one is 94 pages of music long and scene two is 74."

There is only one thing about Charleston and Folly that Mr. Gershwin does not like. "Your amateur composers bring me their pieces for me to play. I am very busy and most of them are very bad – very, very bad," he said.

Heyward took Gershwin on forays to neighboring James Island, which had a large Gullah population. They visited schools and especially churches. Gershwin was particularly fascinated by a dance technique called "shouting," which entailed beating out a complicated rhythm with the feet and hands to accompany the spiritual singing. Heyward wrote:

The most interesting discovery to me, as we sat listening

> to their spirituals ...was that to George it was more like a homecoming than an exploration. The quality in him which had produced the "Rhapsody in Blue" in the most sophisticated city in America, found its counterpart in the impulse behind the music and bodily rhythms of the simple Negro peasant of the South.
>
> I shall never forget the night when at a Negro meeting on a remote sea-island George started 'shouting' with them. And eventually to their huge delight stole the show from their champion 'shouter.' I think he is probably the only white man in America who could have done it.

The first version of the opera ran four hours, with two intermissions, and was performed privately in a concert version at Carnegie Hall in 1935. The world premiere took place at the Colonial Theatre in Boston on September 30, 1935, the traditional out-of-town performance for any show headed for Broadway. The New York opening took place at the Alvin Theatre on October 10, 1935 and ran for 124 performances, impressive for an opera but woefully short for a musical. The reviews were decidedly mixed.

Brooks Atkinson wrote in the *New York Times*, October 9, 1935:

> After eight years of savory memories, *Porgy* has acquired a score, a band, a choir of singers and a new title, Porgy and Bess, which the Theatre Guild put on at the Alvin last evening ... Although Mr. Heyward is the author of the libretto and shares with Ira Gershwin the credit for the lyrics, and although Mr. Mamoulian has again mounted the director's box, the evening is unmistakably George Gershwin's personal holiday ... Let it be said at once that Mr. Gershwin has contributed something glorious to the spirit of the Heywards' community legend.

It was called "crooked folklore and halfway opera" by Virgil Thomson. Whereas, Lawrence Levine stated: "*Porgy and Bess* reflects the odyssey of the African American in American culture." Most critics complained about the form of the show - was it opera or musical?

Gershwin himself anticipated those reactions. In the *New York Times* in 1935 he said:

> Because Porgy and Bess deals with Negro Life in America it brings to the operatic form elements that have never before appeared in the opera and I have adapted my method to utilize the drama, the humor, the superstition, the religious fervor, the dancing and the irrepressible high spirits of the race. If doing this, I have created a new form, which combines opera with theater, this new form has come quite naturally out of the material.

The argument still rages.

George Gershwin. *Courtesy of the George Grantham Bain Collection, Library of Congress*

People in Charleston, however, wasted little time in taking advantage of *Porgy and Bess* for profit. As the first American folk opera, composed by one of America's greatest composers and based on a story written by a native son, the opera was a boon for Charleston marketing. Loutrel Briggs, landscape architect, who had moved to Charleston, became the driving force behind a movement to clean up Cabbage Row. He wanted to save the Row. He wrote:

> DuBose Heyward, with an artistry to which my unskilled pen cannot do justice, has preserved for posterity the picturesque life of "Catfish Row," and I have attempted to reclaim, with as little external change as possible, this building and restore it to something of its original state in revolutionary time.

The Chamber of Commerce paid for the placement of historical markers on structures throughout the city. The 1929 opening of the Cooper River Bridge had given motorists direct access to the city via Route 40 and the Atlantic Coast Highway. There was already an increase of tourists visiting in the city.

The Chicago Tribune wrote:

> In a world of change, Charleston changes less than anything …. Serene and aloof, and above all permanent, it remains a wistful reminder of a civilization that elsewhere has vanished from earth.

With the Great Depression gripping America, Charleston was in no financial position to turn away money. The pre-Revolutionary residential area of Heyward's former neighborhood – Church and Tradd Streets - became a haven for tourist shops, catering to the much-disdained but much-needed Yankee dollar. Ladies of "quality" from Charleston's "first families" opened coffee houses and tea shops and served as "lady guides" on walking tours down the cobblestone streets and back alleys. Their version of Charleston was completely focused on the glory days of the past, discussing "servants" not slaves, architecture not secession, George Washington not Jim Crow. They were trying to preserve, or more realistically, resurrect what Rhett Butler described in *Gone With The Wind:* "the calm dignity life can have when it's lived by gentle folks, the genial grace of days that are gone."

Led by two community-boosting-mayors John P. Grace and Thomas Stoney, this refocusing of history transformed Charleston in the 20ᵗʰ century. The 1930s preservation and tourism campaign solidified Charleston's image as "America's Most Historic City," making it the darling of upscale tourists. In 2012, readers of the international travel magazine *Conde Nast Traveler* voted Charleston the #1 Tourism City in the World.

Broadway production of *Porgy and Bess. Courtesy of the Library of Congress*

Kendra Hamilton wrote:

> The ironies of the situation are compelling. Charleston becomes daily more segregated, the chasm between rich and poor ever deeper and wider, as in the salad days before the war. The tourist-minded city fathers become daily more ingenious at smoothing down the ugly truths of the city's history so as to increase its appeal to people whose impressions of the South owe more to Scarlett O'Hara than Shelby Foote. And yet, the city's most readily identifiable cultural emblems – from Porgy to "the Charleston" – have African-American roots.

During the 1930s and '40s, DuBose Heyward's former home at 76 Church Street became the Porgy Shop. This store sold antiques, china curios and other fine furnishings that had nothing to do with the opera, the play or the novel. It certainly had nothing in common with its namesake, a poor, violent, black beggar turned folk hero.

The Porgy House, 76 Church Street, DuBose Heyward's home, was turned into a gift shop. *Courtesy of the Library of Congress*

In another ironic twist, the "first families" of Charleston, who made money from this skewed, picturesque version of history, did not even allow a version of their most famous commodity to be performed in its home setting until 1970, thirty-four years after its debut. Indeed, Charleston often goes out of its way to soften its African history. In the 1991 video, *Charleston, S.C.: A Magical History Tour*, Mrs. Betty Hamilton, daughter of artist Elizabeth O'Neill Verner, discusses her mother's 1920s-era paintings as capturing "the